D0269670

The Last Post

The Last Post

Music, Remembrance and the Great War

Alwyn W. Turner

Aurum
Press

First published in Great Britain
2014 by Aurum Press Ltd
74—77 White Lion Street
Islington
London N1 9PF
www.aurumpress.co.uk

A catalogue record for this book is available from the British Library.

ISBN 978 1 78131 285 8

1 3 5 7 9 10 8 6 4 2
2014 2016 2018 2017 2015

Typeset in Mrs Eaves by Saxon Graphics Ltd, Derby
Printed and bound by CPI Group (UK) Ltd, Croydon, CR0 4YY

This book is dedicated to my parents
Gordon and Olive Turner,
with love and gratitude,
and to the memory of Joseph Craddock,
who died, aged twenty, at Cambrai in 1917

Contents

Prologue

THE LAST POST

Silent lie our British Isles
On the bosom of the sea;
Silent while two minutes knit
Time unto eternity.

Edward Begbie
'Remembrance' (1919)

W hen Big Ben struck eleven o'clock on the morning of
the 11th of November 1919, no one really knew what
was going to happen next. It was exactly one year since buglers
had sounded the Cease Fire on the Western Front, bringing
the Great War to a close, and just a few days ago King George
V had issued a call that the occasion should be marked by a
moment without precedent or parallel in British history. 'I
believe,' his message proclaimed, 'that my people in every
part of the Empire fervently wish to perpetuate the memory
of that Great Deliverance, and of those who laid down their
lives to achieve it.' And so he proposed that, at 'the eleventh
hour of the eleventh day of the eleventh month, there may be,
for the brief space of two minutes, a complete suspension of
all our normal activities'.

It was a bold idea, and even the King was nervous about its
implementation. How would this work in practice? How
would this 'simple service of Silence and Remembrance'
manifest itself? Above all, how would it feel?

There had been many other commemorations and celebrations and church services in the preceding twelve months, there had been parades and processions, displays of triumph, tribute and thanksgiving, but this was something entirely new. This was not a spectacle, a ceremony conducted by and for the great and the good. It was to be a democratic expression of loss and suffering, in which the entire nation — or so it was hoped — would participate as equals; a suspension, however brief, of social division.

'This is a people's war,' H.G. Wells had written in the early months of the conflict; 'it is not a war for the greater good of British diplomatists, officials and people in uniform. It is our war, not their war, and the last thing we intend to result from it is a permanently increased importance for the military caste.' Now, five long years later, there was to be a symbol of the people's peace, uniting all, regardless of class or age, gender or religion. Not every household in the country was bereaved, but if it had been possible to hold a normal, peacetime funeral for each of the servicemen who had died in the course of the war, then almost everyone would have attended at least one such interment, whether as family or friend. This pause in daily life was an opportunity to reflect the scale of the loss.

But still, no one knew what it would be like. The very nature of the event meant that there would be, could be, hardly any formal organisation. Instructions had been given that all public transport in London should come to a halt, with tube trains remaining in stations so they did not have to sit in tunnels, whilst the Metropolitan Police had been ordered to stop traffic in the capital. Beyond those basic arrangements, however, the government could do little but entrust the implementation of the concept to civic sentiment.

'In factories and workshops it must be left to the good will of employers and employed to make such arrangements as will best carry out the spirit of the scheme,' announced the home secretary, Edward Shortt. 'It is not thought desirable to attempt to close shops or places of business, but shopkeepers and their customers will, it is hoped, agree to a pause during the two minutes' silence.'

Consequently, there was a sense of trepidation. Some worried that the event 'might degenerate into a sort of cheap theatricalism on the one hand, or into a confused and incoherent observance on the other'. Others were cynical about the entire proposition. 'A disgusting idea of artificial nonsense and sentimentality,' snorted the sixteen-year-old Evelyn Waugh in his diary. 'No one thought of the dead last year. Why should they now?' Worst of all, there was the fear that it might not catch the public imagination, that the mood of the nation might have been misjudged.

Even before the chiming of the hour, however, the concerns had been forgotten. The centre of the commemoration was to be the Cenotaph, the temporary wood-and-plaster structure, designed by Edwin Lutyens, that had been erected in Whitehall for the Peace Day parade four months earlier, and which still remained in place. It was now looking a little tired and worn from its unexpectedly prolonged life, but it had already been adopted by the public as their focus for remembrance, and it was there that the greatest crowds congregated. Long before eleven o'clock, the throngs who gathered at the memorial had made the street almost impassable, as it was to stay all day. Flowers had to be passed over people's heads to be placed on the monument, and when the King's wreath, of laurel leaves and yellow immortelles, was sent in a carriage from Buckingham Palace, mounted police had to be called upon to force a passage through the dense press of people.

The King and Queen themselves followed, to be joined by the British prime minister David Lloyd George and the French president Raymond Poincaré, bearing their own wreaths; that of the former was made of laurel leaves adorned with orchids and white roses, and inscribed 'To the Glorious Dead'.

Then, as the eleven chimes of Big Ben began to ring out, the start of the silence was heralded by the firing of maroon signalling rockets from fire stations in the centre of London and from a hundred police stations in the outer boroughs. During the war, maroons had been used to warn of the imminent arrival of German bombers over British cities; now they were again deployed, this time in mourning. The explosion of the rockets startled flocks of pigeons, sending them flying into the air. And, remarkably, the noise of their flapping wings was the only sound to be heard.

For the silence was observed to a degree that many had hoped for, but few had dared dream possible. In an instant, an absolute stillness descended upon the vast crowds at the Cenotaph, a hush so total that the chimes of Big Ben were heard for miles around, in places never before reached in daylight hours. At the centre of the greatest city on Earth, all human activity ceased.

Some fell to their knees at the first signal, clasping their hands in prayer, and remained there throughout. Others stood, heads bowed. Tears fell unchecked, but mostly without noise. As the silence wore on, it was broken only by the muffled weeping of a few of the bereaved, unable to contain their grief, and by the occasional murmur, as when a small boy looked up at his mother, clad all in black, as she stood, her gaze fixed upon the Cenotaph, and whispered to her: 'Is daddy in there, mother?'

Across London, the scene was repeated. In Trafalgar Square, the fountains had been turned off for the duration of the silence and crowds stood motionless. People had gathered too outside the Mansion House, where fifty thousand had attended a short service staged by the Salvation Army, and at St Paul's Cathedral, and in every public square in the city. At the Olympia exhibition centre, the normal business of the Motor Show was halted and 'the only sound in the vast building was the broken sobs of an elderly man in the gallery'. Many shops closed their doors at a quarter to eleven to allow customers to assemble in an orderly fashion. The Lutine Bell, traditionally rung to signify the sinking of a ship, was sounded in Lloyd's of London. In every school, a letter from the King had been read at assembly, and children now stood in silence.

The intensity of the moment, the raw emotions that it conjured up, caught many by surprise. 'There was a loud detonation and immediately the restless traffic was silent, every male head uncovered and all flags on the house-tops slackened in the leech until they were half-mast high,' recorded a serving soldier, who found himself in Oxford Circus. 'For two brief minutes I saw again the distorted horizon of Northern France, and the last resting-place of so many of my gallant comrades. One by one the dearest of them were visualised during those brief two minutes. It was a great and sacred idea.' The solemnity of his experience was shared by a multitude of comrades, both serving and veteran. 'The trams at the termini remained still, and none appeared from the routes,' noted a reporter. 'The drivers and conductors stood around them, and being most of them old Army men, were at attention.'

So total was the observance that any variation, any behaviour that hinted at normality, appeared extraordinary. 'One man walked down Tottenham Court Road during the pause, with the crowd standing bareheaded and the vehicles motionless,' wrote a correspondent, 'and this one man, striding along in the middle of the road, impressed my friend as the strangest apparition he had ever seen. It seemed something against nature.'

In cities, towns and villages across the whole country, the pattern was replicated. It was a freezing cold day, with snowfall and hail in many areas, but few were deterred from marking the occasion. From Cornwall to Caithness, no corner of the land had been untouched by the ravages of the war, and none was yet ready to forget. To inaugurate the silence, maroons were discharged in Bristol, Bradford and Birmingham, artillery fired in Edinburgh and Leeds, church bells rung in rural parts, whilst in Lichfield there was 'the sounding of the siren which was used during the war to give warning of air raids'.

There were civic ceremonies and church services, and for those who could attend neither, there was still the pause as the entire nation came to a standstill. In Belfast 'the sudden hush of great industrial works could almost be felt'. On the packed platforms at Crewe railway station all activity froze, soldiers stood to attention, and 'one old gentleman, who had lost four sons in the war, knelt in silent prayer'. Work stopped in telephone exchanges and telegraph offices, so that the country was 'entirely cut off from the rest of the world'. Court proceedings were suspended to honour the dead, and a smart solicitor in Arbroath, representing two men accused of running a gaming house, took the opportunity to suggest that this might be an appropriate moment for clemency; his argument was sufficiently persuasive that the charges against his clients were dropped.

In Parkhurst Jail, the prison bell was sounded, and the convicts were reported to have observed the silence. So too did three hundred children in the Sailors Orphans Home in Hull, of whom it was noted: 'Most of them were there as a direct result of the war.'

It was a nationwide service, essentially human rather than religious in its spirituality, and it was perhaps the greatest moment of national unity there had ever been, or was ever likely to be. The King's original message had expressed the wish that 'the thoughts of every one may be concentrated on reverent remembrance of the Glorious Dead'. They were. The country came together in a single thought, a single emotion, a single prayer, even if that prayer was addressed to many gods. The idea of such a moment had seemed to some utterly alien and yet when it happened it appeared instantly British. 'It is a strong national trait that we do not carry our hearts on our sleeves,' observed one newspaper, 'and anything like a display of emotion is, and was, particularly in pre-war days, quite foreign to the British character, but the Great War has changed the outlook on many things.'

Nor was the silence confined to Britain. It had its counterpart throughout the Empire, rolling around the world's time zones from New Zealand, through Australia, India and South Africa – where the idea had originally been conceived – to Canada. In Sydney, the crowds gathered in Martin Place, the heart of the city; in Melbourne they congregated outside the Town Hall and Parliament House, then the seat of the federal government: 'both places were in complete silence, and the proverbial pin could be heard to drop.'

Empire and Commonwealth troops around the world, from Belgium to the Black Sea, from Mauritius to Mesopotamia, stood to attention. And on all British ships, flags were dipped and a hush likewise descended. For two minutes the Empire on which the sun never set was in suspended animation.

And then the maroons were fired again, and the silence came to a close. 'It ended with a sigh, and there was a sudden removal of the tension as the crowds began to sway again.' The country returned to its normal business, though it would never afterwards be quite the same. The euphoria that had greeted the Armistice in 1918 had lasted for twelve months, but was now put away. The sobering enormity of what became known as the Great Silence seemed to spell the end of a period in the history of the country, the Empire and the world. Much of what had been lost would never be recaptured.

In the House of Commons the following day, Sir Arthur Steel-Maitland, a Conservative MP for Birmingham, talked of his experience of the silence at Piccadilly Circus. 'One of the most effective things he had ever heard,' it was reported, 'was that during those two minutes he heard very faintly but clearly the sound of the Last Post — he supposed from the Cenotaph in Whitehall.'

He was wrong: there were no buglers to play the Last Post at the Cenotaph that morning. But there were elsewhere, from Westminster Abbey to Selfridges, and across the length and breadth of the country. Those arranging the official commemorations may not have felt the need for the call to be sounded, others clearly did. The enormity of the Silence, the eternity of those two minutes, required release, demanded a moment of cathartic exhalation to channel the emotions of the nation. The sounding of the Last Post could provide that purge.

There was though no consistency, no consensus on how the bugle call was to be used. In Axminster and in Marazion, the Last Post signalled the end of the Silence. In Tamworth the format of military funerals was followed: the Last Post started the Silence, with the call of Reveille to conclude. At Olympia, another call altogether – Stand Fast – was used. Outside the London headquarters of the Australian Army, four buglers sounded Attention and ended the Silence with All Clear, while in Melbourne it was Stand Fast and the Last Post. In Old Machar Cathedral, bugler Edward Milne, formerly of the Gordon Highlanders, played the Cease Fire at the start, and the Last Post and Reveille after.

The nature of remembrance had yet to be agreed, and many elements – the Poppy, the Tomb of the Unknown Warrior, the Festival of Remembrance, the multitude of war memorials – had yet to appear. But the Last Post had a longer history than any of these, and was already well established in public culture. Over the last half-century it had been transformed from its status as just one of dozens of bugle calls heard every day in army camps to become almost a sacred anthem in an increasingly secular country; an inclusive symbol of mourning, beyond religious denomination, beyond nationality. Armistice Day would complete that journey.

Of particular significance was that the people had chosen to embrace the infantry version of the call, played on the humble, functional bugle, rather than the corresponding cavalry call, proclaimed with all the ceremonial splendour of the State Trumpeters. The origins of the infantry's Last Post were unmistakably martial, but this was not the voice of Wells's 'military caste'. It spoke of equality in death, and thereby implied democracy in life. At a time when the establishment and the Empire were looking more fragile than they had for more than a century, when the experience of war seemed to have shaken the very foundations of the nation, the Last Post heralded a new age.

For the unity of the first Silence did not last. It could not last. At best, it could do no more than temporarily conceal the deep divisions in society that the war had exposed and that the peace was to widen. Already the Peace Day parade in July, for which the Cenotaph had been constructed, had sparked riots across the country. There was anger and frustration and bitterness to be felt alongside the sorrow and the celebration of survival. There was a conflict of emotions that would take several years to resolve, but which was already apparent on that first anniversary of Armistice Day. 'The clergy were in scarlet, and were wearing medals as if in thanksgiving for victory,' noted the *Manchester Guardian* of the service held that day in Westminster Abbey. 'But the people, on the anniversary of the day when the war was won, chose but to mourn their dead. After the Last Post, the first verse of the National Anthem was sung as a prayer – there was no note of triumph.'

In the course of the next few years, the rulers of the nation would come into sharp disagreement with the people over how the war was seen, whether it were to be viewed as victory or disaster; whether triumph, grief or restitution should be the dominant note. There was conflict too about what form the symbols of remembrance should take. At stake in that struggle was not only the legacy of the war, but the balance of power in the country, between government and governed. And throughout those troubled times ahead, the Last Post would ring out as a lament for the fallen of the people's war.

On that first commemoration of Armistice Day it was heard, most movingly of all, in the afternoon. For if the

Silence had been staged to remember the dead of the war, then the unofficial ceremony two hours later at the Cenotaph drew attention to the survivors, to those who were still living with their wounds. A small ensemble of former bandsmen led a parade of several hundred disabled ex-servicemen, the blind accompanied by sighted companions, the crippled on crutches. The morning's crowds had not yet dispersed and the procession made all too vividly real the horrors of the conflict. 'This touching spectacle brought tears to the eyes of many of the onlookers,' it was reported. 'Women cried freely. Men stood with faces marked with intense emotion.' As the band played Chopin's 'Marche Funèbre', two of the men stepped forward to lay a wreath to their comrades on the monument. Then came a bagpipe lament and, finally, the playing of the Last Post on solo bugle.

The wounds were not always so visible. Even while the dead were being honoured, there were ex-servicemen facing a bleak future, injured physically and mentally by their experiences on the battlefields, struggling to readjust to civilian life, desperately seeking employment.

In its most extreme form, the psychic damage wreaked on the survivors was seen in Nottingham Assize Court, where proceedings came to a halt at the eleventh hour of the eleventh day of the eleventh month, just as the jury had been sworn in to hear the case against Frederick Carter, a twenty-six-year-old ex-soldier accused of murdering his eighty-year-old landlady, Harriet Shawcroft, with a hatchet. The silence was duly observed, with the prisoner, flanked by two warders, standing rigidly to attention in the dock. Later that afternoon he was sentenced to death. The sentence was subsequently to be commuted, but only because Carter was certified insane and was sent instead to the Broadmoor Criminal Lunatic Asylum.

A workman observes the Silence, high above the Cenotaph

Chapter One

ROUSE

The trumpet's loud clangour
Excites us to arms
With shrill notes of anger
And mortal alarms.

John Dryden
'A Song for St Cecilia's Day' (1687)

The sound of a lone bugler playing the Last Post is one of the most distinctive gifts bequeathed to the world by the British Army. It has spanned the globe, becoming a mournful lament for the dead that has been adopted by governments of all colours, and by individuals and groups of every persuasion: by imperialists and pacifists, by conservatives, communists and fascists, by Christian, Jew, Hindu, Muslim and atheist. No respecter of rank or privilege, it has sounded at the gravesides of millions of soldiers, as well as those of kings and emperors, and of Mohandas Gandhi and Nelson Mandela. It is perhaps best known as the accompaniment to Remembrance Day, but it has never been confined to commemorations of war: it reaches further and deeper than that, part of the national, even of international, culture. Today, when the Tomb of the Unknown Warrior and even the Cenotaph have become too familiar to inspire awe, when the wearing of a poppy has become dulled by routine and the observance of the Silence perfunctory, the sounding of the Last Post retains its power to arrest the soul.

Its origins, however, are a very long way removed from its elevated modern status. It began as a simple bugle call, sounded each and every day as part of army routine and signifying nothing more than that the camp's perimeter had been secured for the night. Over the course of a century or so, it took on additional meaning and weight, first as the accompaniment to a soldier's funeral, then as a memorial for the dead, before being adopted by the civilian population and accepted as the music of remembrance. Perhaps it is those long roots, or perhaps simply the evocative nature of music, but the Last Post enjoys a unique, almost sacred status, virtually untouched by the attention of satirists and comedians. This anonymous melody is the most powerful piece of folk music Britain has ever produced.

The bugle is a comparatively recent addition to the musical instrumentation of the British Army, introduced only in the last decades of the eighteenth century. Its name, however, derived from *bos*, the Latin word for an ox, suggests the long ancestry of the instrument. From the earliest times, humans had discovered the sounds to be made from blowing through the hollowed-out horns of animals, sometimes those of oxen, antelopes or bulls, sometimes – as in the case of the Israelite forces led by Joshua before the walls of Jericho – those of rams. In most instances, these sounds were put to use in military and ceremonial functions.

The natural extension to the practice of using found instruments was to construct them, to replicate nature in metal, thereby allowing for the development of uniformity in tuning. This evolution from horn to trumpet was not confined to a single culture, and wind instruments of bronze, copper or silver were known throughout the ancient world, in Egypt, Mesopotamia, China and Greece. They were known too in Britain. When the Roman armies arrived in the first century AD, they were met by Celtic forces who used the carnyx, a long S-shaped trumpet made of bronze that was held vertically, so that the mouthpiece was the lowest point and the sound came out of a bell — typically in the form of a boar or a serpent — some ten feet off the ground. Rising out of the morning mist, as the Celts charged into battle, the carnyx was a weapon of war, intended to strike fear into the enemy with its harsh, blasting noise and its fearsome appearance.

The carnyx, however, did not survive, and it was the Romans whose influence was to shape musical developments in Britain. They used a variety of bronze and copper instruments, some straight, up to four and a half feet in length, some curved; but more importantly they used them for military functions beyond mere aggression. The trumpet, it was discovered, could be blown to control tactics on the battlefield, and to regulate the everyday life of the soldier. 'Their times also for sleeping and watching and rising are notified beforehand by the sound of trumpets,' wrote the historian Josephus, describing the Roman army in the first century AD, 'nor is any thing done without such a signal.'

These instruments — known retrospectively as natural trumpets to distinguish them from their modern descendants — remained largely the same over the centuries: simple cylinders of metal, with a mouthpiece at one end, a bell at the other, and no holes, keys or valves to vary the pitch; that was achieved solely through the embouchure of the player, squeezing notes out of the instrument by tightening the lips when blowing. The longer the tube, the greater the range of harmonics available, and therefore the more subtle the music that could be played.

A thousand years on from the Roman departure from Britain, little had changed in terms of trumpets, though new military instruments were being introduced. In 'The Knight's Tale', Geoffrey Chaucer wrote of:

> Pypes, trompes, nakers, clariounes
> That in the bataille blowen blody sounes

while Edward III's victory over the Scots at Halidon Hill in 1333 was commemorated in a ballad that made specific reference to the instruments deployed by the English:

> This was to do with merry sowne,
> With pipes, trumpes and tabers thereto,
> And loud clarions thei blew also.

Tabers — more normally spelt tabors — and nakers were early forms of side-drum and kettle-drum respectively, first encountered in the ranks of the Saracen armies during the Crusades. There was a clear division between the two, reflecting a traditional and long-lived class distinction in the army. The kettle-drum, along with the trumpet, was increasingly reserved for the elite regiments of cavalry, employed for ceremonial functions and associated with royalty; the side-drum was used by the more lowly infantry.

By the beginning of the seventeenth century, drums had taken on three distinct military functions. They beat out time for an army on the march; they communicated orders on the battlefield; and they marked out the passage of the day in camp. The last of these roles was perhaps the least appreciated in civilian society, but it was where the greatest impact was made on the psyche of the soldier, establishing a diurnal rhythm that shaped military life. The camp was roused at daybreak by the beating of Reveille, and it closed down at night with a sequence of two beats that were known collectively as Tattoo: first came a signal that the officer of the watch had commenced his inspection of the sentry points; then, some thirty minutes later, a final beat as the inspection concluded and the camp was declared secure for the night. The word 'Tattoo' gave some indication of the recreational preferences of the British soldier; it was borrowed from the Dutch *doe den tap-toe*, an instruction to turn off the beer taps in taverns at the end of the evening, and the first beating served as an order to those drinking outside the barracks that it was time to return.

The cavalry, meanwhile, were evolving their own set of trumpet calls for use in camp, with a repertoire in the seventeenth century of six calls: Butte Sella, Mounte Cavallo, A la Standarde, Tuquet, Carga and Aquet, the last of which – also known as the Watch – was used both first thing in the morning and last thing at night.

The numbers of such calls steadily increased so that by the mid-eighteenth century there were fifteen different drum beats used either on the battlefield or in camp, but in both arenas the limitations of the drum were becoming increasingly apparent. With medieval weaponry replaced by muskets, manoeuvrable cannon and finally rifles, the sound of a drum struggled to be heard in conflict, while the lack of variation in tone meant that there was a finite number of beats that a soldier could be expected to remember. And so, in place of the drum, came the bugle-horn, introduced during the reign of George III and adapted from a type of bugle used by the Hanoverian military.

The structure of the new instrument differed in several key respects from the existing cavalry trumpet. Where the trumpet was cylindrical for almost its entire length, before flaring out into the bell, the tube of a bugle was conical from mouthpiece to horn, giving a more abrasive, less mellifluous sound. The piping was shorter and – at this early stage – was coiled into a circular shape or curved into a half-moon like a hunting horn, making it a more compact instrument, suitable for carrying on the march. The familiar modern shape of the bugle, wound twice around and looking akin to an unkeyed cornet, was to follow in the first half of the nineteenth century, though the image of the original shapes survived on the cap badges of several regiments. Still without keys or valves, it was restricted to five or six notes, but even so offered far greater flexibility than a drum.

This was an instrument for a new age, functional rather than ceremonial, its stubby shape speaking of humble utilitarianism rather than showy ostentation. There was no room on the restricted length of a bugle for hanging a banner. It lacked the elongated elegance and aristocratic bearing of the cavalry trumpet, and it replaced the rich, sonorous tones with a brash, shrill urgency. In short, it looked and sounded as though it were designed for the industrial revolution not for the Restoration court.

It was also perfectly suited to a new style of warfare in which mobility was a prized attribute, and its arrival coincided with the development of the light infantry in the British Army, regiments of riflemen who were to make their name in the Napoleonic Wars. Even before that conflict, however, a battalion of such troops was to be seen in Hyde Park in 1777, practising its manoeuvres before embarking for service in the American Revolutionary War, and being 'regulated by the sound of a bugle-horn'. A report from the following year similarly emphasised this use of the instrument to control soldiers: 'The movements of the Light Brigade are performed, with amazing address and agility, to the sound of a bugle-horn.' It was with the light infantry that the bugle was to become particularly associated, so that a soldier serving in the Peninsular War with the 95th (Rifle) Regiment could boast that 'the buglers of his regiment formed a band over twenty strong'.

Its use, however, was not restricted to these ranks. Bugles sounded the advance as Wellington's army left camp for the battle of Waterloo, and had by then even been adopted by some cavalry regiments, most notably the Scots Greys. In so doing, of course, they were blurring the distinction that had grown up between the instrumentation of the infantry and that of the cavalry, a fact that attracted official disapproval. In 1835 British cavalry regiments were prohibited from using bugles, though the ban was not to last: the size of cavalry trumpets made them less practical on the battlefield, their lower pitch meant their calls did not pierce the noise of conflict in the way that bugles could, and the greater range of notes made mistakes more likely. Consequently a variant on the bugle was produced, with the same length of tubing but more loosely coiled into a longer, more elegant shape.

The emergence of the infantry bugle necessitated the adoption of a fresh set of calls, since those used by the trumpet could not be played on the new instrument, and the period of transition was not without problems. Perhaps the most risky of all calls was Parley, played when approaching enemy lines for the purposes of negotiating. This was the one signal that needed to be understood not only by the player's comrades but also by his adversaries, and the shift from trumpet to bugle was fraught with danger: in 1778 a British detachment found itself under fire from the French at St Lucia when the new bugle Parley was not recognised. (In later years a different problem arose. During the Boer War it was reported that, in a distinctly underhand trick, 'the Boers had learned our bugle calls' and played the Cease Fire to confuse the British troops.)

It was largely in response to such episodes, and as part of a wider push towards conformity across the Army, that in 1798 James Hyde, trumpet major of the London and Westminster Dragoons and a trumpeter in the orchestra of the Covent Garden Opera House, was asked to lead an inquiry into the various calls that were then being used. The stated intention was 'to revise the trumpet and bugle soundings, and to reduce them to uniformity, which is hereafter to be strictly observed in all regiments and corps of cavalry in His Majesty's service'. Hyde was paid the not inconsiderable sum of thirty pounds for his work, and the results were published later that year, effectively spelling the demise of the drum as the preferred instrument for signalling orders in combat; the battlefield use of the drum survived, but henceforth it was primarily employed for purposes of morale. Unfortunately the document that resulted from Hyde's endeavours, *The Sounds for Duty and Exercise*, was so riddled with errors and typographical mistakes that it was of little immediate use, and in 1799 he published his own version with the addition of 'The Bugle Horn Duty for the Light Infantry as used in the Foot Guards'. Included therein was the call that would later become famous as the Last Post, but which was then known under the title Setting the Watch, the bugle equivalent of Tattoo.

The antiquity, let alone the authorship, of the piece is entirely lost, though the call almost certainly predates Hyde and the cavalry version may have been well over a century old by this stage. It has been speculated that the long melodic lines of infantry calls like Reveille and the Last Post, reaching far beyond simple repetitions, might indicate that they were assembled from several sources, a compilation of calls from different regiments, possibly put together by Hyde. Others have argued that the subtlety of these pieces suggests the hand of an experienced composer, with the name of Joseph Haydn being mentioned. Haydn had recently been a huge success on his two visits to London, during the latter of which (in 1794–5) he wrote his Military Symphony, featuring fanfare trumpets, but there is nothing to link him directly to the bugle calls published by James Hyde.

Setting the Watch was to remain the official name of the call for well over half a century. A book titled *Barrack Calls for Sappers and Miners*, published in 1850, was still listing Setting the Watch: 1st Post and Setting the Watch: 2nd Post, and it was not until the King's Regulations of 1873 that there was the first official reference to what was now called the Last Post of Tattoo. Common usage, however, had already renamed the call by that point, as an account of 'Life in a Barrack' from a decade earlier made clear:

> Tattoo is divided into the First Post and Last Post. The First Post sounds at nine, when all the men's names are called in the barrack-rooms; the names of those who are absent being taken down. As many men as return before the Last Post has sounded, at half-past nine, have their names scratched from the list, which is then taken up to the orderly officer. As the absentees drop in they are marched to the guard-room, which is pretty full by midnight, with deserters, absentees and men drunk.

The timings varied. Officially the First Post was to be sounded at nine o'clock in winter and at ten o'clock in summer, but, depending on local circumstances and preferences, it could be later still. And the Last Post — despite its name — was not the final call of the day: it was followed fifteen, or sometimes thirty, minutes later by the brief sounding of Lights Out. The man who played these calls would then sleep in the guard-house, so he could be woken next morning in time to sound Reveille, the first call of the day.

The number of signals grew still further with the advent of the bugle. The schedule for a Rifle Volunteers encampment at Woodsome, Yorkshire, in 1873 showed a daily routine of twenty-six calls. Then there were the other calls heard infrequently in camp (Alarm, Fire Alarm) and a further set that were used on the battlefield. 'There are altogether over sixty different calls in constant use,' noted an officer in 1885. There were also calls specific to each regiment and battalion, sometimes to each company too, which were played immediately before the main call, to inform soldiers in action that they were being addressed directly.

Apart from the obvious function of ensuring that soldiers were in the right place at the right time in an era when few possessed watches, there was a psychological dimension to the sounding of the daily calls, reminding those serving of their place in a larger machine. 'All bugle calls denote that a soldier's life is a watch and a vigil,' Stephen Graham, who served in the Scots Guards during the First World War, was later to reflect. 'He does not go by the clock, or claim any time as his own, but gives obedience instant upon the demand of his superior. The bugle call is the voice of the King.'

There was, in the first half of the nineteenth century, no special meaning or resonance to the Last Post that might distinguish it from all the other calls heard daily by serving soldiers. In later years, there would be much talk of its eerie, haunting nature, but this was not how it was perceived by those whose days were marked out by the duty bugler. Its associations were not with death and remembrance, but rather with the end of the evening's revelry, and therefore all too often with a temporary suspension of the pleasurable pursuits of drinking, gambling and whoring that made a soldier's life worth living. In Valletta, Malta, there was for a long time a custom whereby 'buglers toured hostelries playing the First Post at the first inn, and the Last Post at the last'. Elsewhere it was reported that 'The Tattoo or First Post may be heard at 9.30 pm and is not unfrequently followed by a roll of drums, and then a marching through the streets by the drum and fife band.' The Last Post was an instrument of discipline, and it wasn't welcomed with the same enthusiasm that greeted, say, 'the glorious "grog" call, or the call for meat and drink and bread to be served out'.

During peacetime, the ubiquity of the calls in camp ensured that over-familiarity bred contempt, or at least good-natured disrespect. There were official words attached to the calls, to assist soldiers in remembering them, but they were seldom used. Few cared for the authorised words for Rouse — ending with 'Get out of bed, it's past Reveille! Get out now, sharp for the day's begun' — when the alternative was so much more memorable: 'Get out of bed, get out of bed, get out of bed, you lazy buggers!' And well into the twentieth century the call for Officers' Mess was accompanied by an ancient piece of doggerel:

> Officers' wives have puddings and pies
> But sergeants' wives have skilly,
> And the private's wife has nothing at all
> To pack her poor little belly.

Skilly, a particularly unappetising form of oatmeal gruel, had long since disappeared from the army menu, and was now served only to convicts, but in any event the mention of food was merely a metaphor for the soldier's perennial preoccupation with sex.

There were no such ribald words associated with the Last Post, but not because its status was too revered for parody. For many years, a standard practical joke played on a new recruit, the military equivalent of a left-handed hammer or a tin of striped paint in industry, was to send him to the guardhouse to ask the sergeant for a brush so that he might complete his task of whitewashing the Last Post. There was nothing sacrosanct about any particular call.

During times of conflict, on the other hand, the calls acquired greater authority, conveying a sense of continuity and stability in soldiers' lives, despite the changed circumstances. 'At nine, infantry bugles in vessels three miles at sea blew the Last Post to recall stragglers, with as much regularity as if still in barracks at Winchester or Portsmouth,' wrote a correspondent, attached to the British forces in the Crimea in 1854, 'and at midnight the silver trumpets from cavalry transports wound clear and long their melancholy notes, proclaiming to the assembled squadrons that none of their men were absent.'

There were other calls too that took on deeper, more profound significance, depending on the situation in which they were played. Following the fall of Kabul in 1841 during the First Anglo-Afghan War, the garrison at Jalalabad, some hundred miles or so from the capital, waited anxiously for the expected arrival of the sixteen thousand-strong retreating force under General William Elphinstone. Just one man came, Dr William Brydon, staggering in through the gates and claiming that he was the sole survivor of what had turned into a massacre. Unwilling to give up hope, the commanding officer at Jalalabad instructed his buglers to take up post on the city walls at dusk to play the Advance and Assembly, in order to let any other stragglers and survivors know that there was safe haven to be found. In the words of Sergeant Edward Teer of the 13th Light Infantry, then serving in the garrison, their task was 'To send the message of welcome and safety ringing over those barren plains and amongst those pitiless hills, to sound those clear and stirring notes which would have been so gladly heard by those whom death had made silent for ever.' For six nights the 'resurrection bugles', as they were dubbed in the garrison, played their lonely, pitiful call, the sound muffled by the thick snow, until finally it was accepted that it was all in vain, that no further survivors were forthcoming: 'we ceased to hope that stragglers from the vanished army would answer the call, and after that the bugles rang no more.'

In different circumstances, it was Reveille, the first call of the day, that appeared 'the most poetic of the bugle calls'. On hearing it on board a ship in 1894, a reporter wrote of its haunting quality when encountered in a fleet, each ship's bugler a fraction out of time with the others: 'there is produced one of the Reveille's greatest, if unintentional charms, a melange of music, the tune of one's own ship predominating, frequently the solitary bugler of a very small ship lagging behind in dispute with the echo.' Another journalist wrote of 'the beautiful but weirdlike Reveille', and remembered the morning of the battle of Tamai, when British units routed Mahdist forces in Eastern Sudan: 'All night we had lain silent while the enemy cracked volleys of musketry into us from the bush outside our zerebah. But with the first Reveille we sprang to our feet as one man, glad all of us to think that now our turn had come.'

There were others, those in the ranks, who found cruelty not beauty in the early-morning call. 'The Reveille had sounded,' remembered Sergeant Patrick Conway of the Royal Artillery, as he recalled the battle of Inkerman in 1854, 'but the ring of the bugle was almost a mockery to famished and disease-stricken troops who had been so long on duty in the trenches that sleep was nearly a forgotten blessing.'

Little of this culture of army life, however, meant very much in wider British society. For centuries, the populace had regarded soldiers with suspicion and mistrust, and even the presence of an army in peacetime was a source of political dispute. 'They are a body of men distinct from the body of the people,' argued the Whig MP William Pulteney in 1732; 'they are governed by different laws; blind obedience and an entire submission to the orders of their commanding officer is their only principle.'

Following the upheavals of the Civil War, misgivings were so great that for nearly two hundred years the Mutiny Act, first passed in 1689, had to be renewed annually by Parliament in order to permit the continued existence of a standing army. Such an institution was considered by many to be essentially alien and hostile to British civil liberties, a perception strengthened by the fact that, until the Napoleonic Wars, the army included large numbers of foreign mercenaries from Germany and the Low Countries. There were few British families with even one representative in the ranks, and the life of the private soldier was held in low public esteem, the last refuge of the desperate and the near-criminal. Soldiers enlisted for twenty-one years, and during their service were regarded as a brawling, drunken imposition on the country; after their discharge, they were frequently to be observed begging and living rough on the streets.

Trumpeter George Gritten and twelve-year-old bugler William Lang of
the Royal Artillery pose with trophies from the Crimean War

At times of great victories, the commanders and generals – whether Marlborough, Wolfe or Wellington – might be feted and honoured, but the other ranks were seen as a necessary evil at best, and few were concerned with the conditions in which they served. The description of the troops famously attributed to the Duke of Wellington, that they were 'the scum of the earth', was an accurate reflection of popular opinion, and it was tacitly understood that draconian discipline was needed to control such men. When, in the early nineteenth century, the Duke of York – the son of George III, and the Commander-in-Chief of the Army – attempted to reform the brutal system of military punishment by imposing a maximum sentence of three hundred lashes, he found little support amongst either senior officers or civilians, and had to settle for a compromise that if a man fell unconscious during a beating, it would cease.

The traditional attitudes to the regular soldier took a long time to die within the Army, as George Dunlop, who served in the Abyssinian War of 1867–8, remembered: 'Our Commander-in-Chief was a stern soldier of those earlier days when men were considered simply as fighting machines, and when the private was looked upon as being something that was scarcely to be accounted human.'

By then, however, a change in public sentiment was becoming apparent. It began with the Crimean War of 1854–6, a conflict that saw Britain and France send forces to curb Russian expansionism, as the Ottoman Empire began to wane. This was the first major military confrontation since Waterloo, some four decades earlier, and was greeted initially with popular enthusiasm. It was also the first war to be covered by newspapers at a time when the press was gaining rapidly in influence: in 1815 *The Times* had had a circulation of just fifteen thousand;

now, assisted by developments in printing technology, that figure had risen to over forty thousand, while the advent of the telegraph enabled more rapid coverage of foreign affairs. The paper was represented in the Crimea by the Irish journalist William Howard Russell, who spent two years with the Army and created the trade of war correspondent, fraternising with junior officers and other ranks and reporting on the campaign with a frankness that shocked his readers at home.

Amongst his early successes was his coverage of a decision taken at the start of hostilities to ban all music, including the sounding of bugles, in British camps, out of a misguided belief that such signals might reveal positions and strengths to the enemy. For professional soldiers, whose lives had been regulated and disciplined by the everyday routine of the calls, the sudden absence was disorientating and distressing. Nor was the change successful in achieving its aims, particularly since no such ban was enforced amongst Britain's allies. 'The silence and gloom of our camp, as compared with the activity and bustle of that of the French, are very striking,' reported Russell. 'No drum, no bugle-call, no music of any kind is ever heard within our precincts, while our neighbours close by keep up incessant rolls, fanfaronnades and flourishes, relieved every evening by the fine performances of their military bands.' He concluded that, 'judging from one's own feelings, and from the expressions of those around, the want of music in camp is productive of graver consequences than appear likely to occur at first blush'. Largely as a result of his dispatches, the prohibition was lifted.

More widely, Russell's reporting drew public attention to the appalling conditions endured by soldiers. Many years after the conflict, Fergus Farrow, who had served in the Land Transport Corps, reflected on his experiences in the Crimea.

'Our men died like so many sheep, and it was pitiful to hear the cries of the wounded and disease-stricken, for whom so little could be done,' he recalled. 'It was terrible, and sometimes the memory of it haunts me like a nightmare. The discipline was of the strictest. I frequently saw poor fellows flogged for relatively slight offences, and they were punished unmercifully for any misdeed. The wonder is any of us lived through it.' Just over twenty thousand did not survive, and of those the great majority, perhaps as many as eight in every ten, died not on the battlefield or of their wounds, but of disease.

This was, perhaps, the greatest revelation for the British public: that away from the glory and valour of the battlefield, the worst horrors were to be found in the care – or lack of it – afforded to troops. It came as something of a revelation to those who had previously regarded the soldier as no more than a disreputable ruffian to see him portrayed instead as a victim of bureaucratic incompetence.

The impact could be seen in the reporting of the first war memorial of the conflict, a sculpture by Carlo Marochetti that was ultimately to be installed at the Crystal Palace, and that was announced in the early summer of 1855, even as hostilities continued. Initiated by Florence Nightingale, whose work at the military hospital in Scutari was inspiring the nation, the piece was intended as a monument to those who had died in that institution, a 'tribute of respect to the memory of so many brave men, the victims of disease and neglect', as the newspapers put it. The following year, after the British government had fallen and a new administration had signed the Treaty of Paris to end the war, it was proposed to build an Anglican church in Constantinople which, as well as 'affording a witness of the true faith to the Mahomedan', would stand as a memorial to the dead. 'It is a pleasing, yet melancholy, fact,' the press noted, 'that the name of every one of those gallant countrymen, whose lives fell a sacrifice to the calls of military duty during the late war, will be inscribed in the vaulted chamber beneath the Memorial Church – so that the edifice will be a monument and record of those who died in the Crimean campaign.'

In the event, the Crimea Memorial Church, consecrated in 1868, did not feature a list of names as proposed, but the very fact that such an idea was being voiced marked a major change in the British public's image of the soldier. In the past, victory had been celebrated through the veneration of the great man to whom the nation was grateful for its triumph; as recently as the 1840s, Nelson's Column had been erected in the newly laid-out Trafalgar Square. Although that custom was not brought to an end by the Crimean War, it was significantly augmented. No longer was it sufficient to erect a statue to the commander or general; now there was an acknowledgement of the equality brought by death, the great leveller.

A memorial to the Royal Engineers at Brompton Barracks in London listed 'the names of every officer and man who fell in the Crimea', whilst at the Royal Victoria Hospital near Southampton a monument sixty feet high was erected, 'recording the names of the medical officers who fell in the Crimean War'. The public schools too wished to remember their losses and in 1856 a meeting of Old Etonians voted 'That memorial windows of those Etonians who had fallen in the Crimean war should be placed in the chapel of Eton College.' More symbolic still was the placement of a stone in the churchyard in Balmaclellan, near Dumfries, which bore the names and details of five men from the village who had died in the Crimea. Similar monuments were erected in Beeston, Nottinghamshire, in Southam, Warwickshire, and

The Memorial Arch at Chatham to the men of the Royal Engineers
who died during the Crimean War

in Holywell, Flintshire. These were civic memorials, not
regimental or institutional, and they commemorated the
contributions of the rank-and-file, the ordinary soldier not
the general.

In a parallel development, the Victoria Cross was created
in 1856 (and backdated to the start of the Crimean campaign)
to commemorate acts of bravery and courage regardless of
rank or class, the first time that such an award had been
open to both officers and men. Amongst the early recipients
were Andrew Henry, the principal keyed-bugle player of the
Royal Artillery, and bugler William Sutton of the 60th

Rifles. The inauguration of the Victoria Cross was again a sign of an increased public and official interest in the contribution of troops beyond the upper reaches of the officer class.

Meanwhile, the most celebrated cultural work of the conflict was Alfred, Lord Tennyson's 'The Charge of the Light Brigade' (1854), an account of the catastrophic action during the battle of Balaclava. Tennyson's lines acknowledged that 'Someone had blundered', but the poem chiefly became famous for celebrating heroism in the face of impossible odds:

> Theirs not to make reply,
> Theirs not to reason why,
> Theirs but to do and die.

Thus were made a virtue precisely those characteristics of 'blind obedience' that William Pulteney had complained of more than a century earlier, now perceived as selfless sacrifice and, as such, requiring recognition and respect.

It was a time of contradictory developments in Britain: abroad, the Empire was still growing, but so too was democracy at home. The 1832 Reform Act had provided the first hesitant steps towards extending the franchise, while the Chartist movement – reaching its peak in 1848 – had shown that the pressure for further change could not be indefinitely resisted. A new public understanding of the Army suited the national mood. The Crimean War, the conflict that first gave rise to the phrase 'lions led by donkeys', began the process of transforming the 'scum of the earth' into national heroes, inaugurating – if a little tentatively – the modern era of remembrance and commemoration.

'The present war is a people's war,' *The Times* had declared in an editorial in 1854, anticipating H.G. Wells by sixty years, and for the first time it seemed that at least some of the people were to be recognised.

Chapter Two
GENERAL SALUTE

The day's high work is over and done,
And these no more will need the sun:
Blow, you bugles of England, blow!
These are gone whither all must go,
Mightily gone from the field they won.

W.E. Henley
'The Last Post' (1900)

Perhaps appropriately for an instrument that seemed to belong to an era of industrialised democracy rather than to the rarefied circles of a royal court, the bugle was never favoured by the great composers. Largely, of course, that omission was a consequence of the instrument's limited range. The natural trumpet, on the other hand – the family to which the E-flat cavalry trumpet belongs, and of which it is now almost the sole survivor – was likewise without valves, but its greater length allowed for more subtlety; its tonal and melodic possibilities were exploited with varying degrees of success by Bach, Handel, Mozart and Beethoven, as well as by Haydn. Even within the world of military music, the bugle has seldom been much celebrated. Marches for bands comprised of bugles and drums have been written in great number, but none has made an impact on a wider public in the same way as those by the likes of John Philip Sousa, Kenneth J. Alford or Julius Fučik.

From a British perspective, the one exception, the one piece in the bugle's repertoire that has achieved instant recognition, is the Last Post. It is 'a British gift to the world which both Purcell and Handel might have been proud to have composed', wrote Francis Boyd, the distinguished political journalist, adding that its 'magic is universal, not solely British'.

The power of the piece resides not in its origins as a signal that the inspection of the night-watch posts had been completed, but in the use to which it was later to be put, at funerals and services of remembrance. 'Few things are more impressive than a military funeral,' observed the *Manchester Guardian* in 1905. 'There are the solemn notes of the Dead March in *Saul*, the coffin covered by a Union Jack borne on a gun carriage, the measured tramp of comrades following, the rattle of the farewell volleys fired over the grave, and the weird sound of the Last Post.' A century, even a half-century, earlier and that description of the Last Post as 'weird' would have been unthinkable; as late as 1899 it was still being described as 'one of the most difficult of calls and one of the prettiest'. It is the associations that subsequent generations have laid on the piece that have given it its elegiac tones.

Music had long been part of military funerals, the sound of muffled drums accompanying burials from the sixteenth century onwards. The association of the drum with death was evident too in the legend of Cortachy Castle, the seat of the Earls of Airlie in Scotland, which was said to be haunted by the ghost of a drummer boy. Having offended his master, the boy had been sewn into a drum and thrown from the highest tower to his death, and his spectral reappearance, beating

Tattoo, was believed to herald a death in the family. It was not until the 11th Earl was killed in action in the Boer War in 1900, with no sign of the drummer's ghost, that the curse was lifted. (Coincidentally, at around the same time, a story grew up that a bugler had fallen to his death while sounding the Last Post from the roof of the military school of music at Kneller Hall; his ghost too was reputed to haunt the place.)

To the drums was added the bugle, and its emergence at military funerals can be traced through the vogue that existed, both during and after the wars with revolutionary France, for slightly mawkish poems bearing the title 'The Soldier's Funeral'. An early example was one of the pieces included in Charles Dibdin's *Castles in the Air* (1793), which makes no mention of the instrument, speaking instead of:

> The plaintive fife and muffl'd drum
> The man may summon to his silent home.

Other variations on the same theme over the next two decades are similarly silent on the subject of bugles. It is not until after the defeat of Napoleon that they make their appearance, as in this anonymous verse published in 1821:

> I heard the roll of muffled drum –
> I heard the bugle's lonely wailing –
> As to the churchyard they were come
> With honours naught availing.

and again in William Miller's piece, also titled 'The Soldier's Funeral', published in *The Fairy Minstrel and Other Poems* the following year:

How sadly sublime is the bugle's wild breath!
And how mournful the funeral train!
To prove that the Soldier is honour'd at death,
Tho' he fall not to sleep with the slain.

The subject of the soldier's funeral — contrasting the tranquillity of death with the exertions of war — remained fashionable amongst amateur poets for another twenty years, and the bugle is omnipresent from this point onwards. It was not, however, playing the Last Post, and the more prosaic newspaper reports of funerals in the same era tend to emphasise not the 'lonely wailing' or the 'sadly sublime' sound, but rather the harsh, penetrating pitch of the instrument. 'After the service was completed the sergeants loaded their rifles with blank cartridge, and fired three volleys into the air. The shrill tone of the bugle was the signal for each volley,' read one such account, while at the funeral of Lord Palmerston, the former prime minister, in 1865 'the sudden sound of a bugle shrilly broke the silence'.

Along with the three volleys (fired, according to soldierly superstition, to scare off the devil and keep him from claiming the dead man's soul), most of the musical elements of a military funeral were in place by the end of the eighteenth century: the muffled drums, the instruments draped in black crepe, and the stately solemnity of the Dead March from Act III of Handel's 1738 oratorio *Saul*, which had become a fixture at royal interments and which has been played over the centuries to mark the passing of heroes from Horatio Nelson to Nelson Mandela. But it is not until the second half of the nineteenth century that the first report in print is to be found of the Last Post in such a context, and then it is not in Britain.

In 1853 the Reverend W.B. Clark of the Free Church of Scotland was, somewhat against his will, instructed to leave his ministry in Maxwelltown, Kirkcudbrightshire, to take up a position in Quebec. Feeling homesick and 'disheartened at the dreary appearance of the country', where 'the great body of the inhabitants are of another race, another religion and another language', he took to writing long letters back to his hometown newspaper, the *Dumfries and Galloway Standard*. It was in one of these letters, dated the 5th of October 1853, that he told of the funeral of a Scottish soldier named Burns from Forfar, who was serving in the 71st Regiment (Highland) Light Infantry and who had died of disease:

> When the coffin was deposited in the grave, the Last Post was played between every volley that was fired over it. There is something touching and appropriate in this. The Last Post is the call that is played at night after all the soldiers are supposed to be in their rooms. And when the soldier is placed in his long home, what music so appropriate as the Last Post. But there is a day coming when tones of a trumpet more solemn will be heard, and a reveille will be sounded which will not fail to rouse every sleeper.

The fact that Clark felt the need to explain the custom and its meaning makes it clear that this was not common practice at home. There is in his account a suggestion of invention born of necessity. The 71st were a much-travelled regiment, at a time when it was difficult to persuade military musicians and bandmasters (many of whom were then civilians) to venture overseas; with the paucity of music available in an isolated camp in a foreign land, it appears that a bugle was pressed into rough and ready service. Clark's letter, with its reference to the Day of Judgement, also implies that there was no sounding of Reveille at the graveside, for surely he would otherwise have mentioned it.

More than a decade would pass before an equivalent use of the Last Post was heard on British soil. The earliest recorded occasion was the 1871 burial in Elswick Cemetery, Newcastle, of Lieutenant-Colonel Henry Christian All-husen, who had served in the Newcastle Artillery Volunteer Corps. The band of this unit, forty strong and under the leadership of Bandmaster J.H. Amers, played at the funeral. 'At the grave the usual volleys were fired,' noted the *Newcastle Guardian and Tyne Mercury*, 'and between the first and second the band played [William] Morley's chant in D minor, and after the third volley they played the Last Post on trumpets only. The whole service was of a most impressive character.' The reference to trumpets is almost certainly misleading, for although there was a well-established Last Post that was played on trumpets in the cavalry, a rival newspaper wrote that the 'ceremony closed with the blowing of the bugle call the Last Post', and it seems much more likely that it was the infantry version, played on bugles, that was heard at Allhusen's interment.

From the 1880s onwards, the call became increasingly common at such ceremonies, as the practice gradually passed into convention. Typical of many was the funeral of drummer John James at Alnwick, Northumberland, in 1888: 'before the grave was closed three volleys were fired over it and the long mournful wail of the Last Post blown.' The custom was far from universal, however. Later the same year, at the funeral of Armoury-Sergeant Drew in Gloucester Barracks, 'three volleys were fired over the grave by the escort, the band rendering a portion of the Reveille between each volley'. And there were variations to be heard for decades to come, so that when Bandmaster Percy Battishill, who had served in the Royal Artillery, was buried in 1924 in Shoeburyness, Essex, the First Post was sounded at the graveside and then, after the customary three volleys were fired, came the Last Post.

The more normal pattern that emerged, however, was the sounding of the Last Post, to symbolise the ending of earthly life, followed by a period of silent prayer, and then the playing of Reveille, the first call of the morning, to suggest the soul's awakening to a new day, a rebirth into eternal life.

It was a simple and highly effective metaphor taken from the daily routine of the soldier, and it is surely no coincidence that the tradition of playing the Last Post at funerals followed shortly on from the call acquiring its modern name. For decades under the older version of the title – Setting the Watch: 2nd Post – there had been no such practice. Nor was it a straightforward adoption of the final evening call, since more commonly that would have been Lights Out, rather than the Last Post. It was all in the name. It was the echo of the phrase 'the last trump', from St Paul's First Letter to the Corinthians, with its promise of resurrection on Judgement Day, that made the association so powerful.

And, as it evolved, it was also about the playing. The tempo of the Last Post when used at funerals was slowed down considerably from its everyday incarnation. Notes were held much longer, pauses were emphasised. There was a degree of pathos, of yearning mournfulness and loss, that was not inherent in the music as written. It was already one of the longer calls and when sounded at night would last around forty-five seconds; played slowly at a funeral, that could be extended by thirty seconds, without the addition of any further material.

Twelve-year-old bugler Gustav A. Schurmann, who served in the
Union Army in the American Civil War

The evolution of the Last Post from daily signal to funeral lament in Britain was paralleled at around the same time in America. There too a bugle was used to denote key moments of the day, the calls employed including one titled Tattoo, published in an 1835 military manual by Winfield Scott and therefore known as the Scott Tattoo. It was, like all American calls of the era, borrowed directly from the repertoire of the French revolutionary army, but in July 1862, during the Peninsular Campaign of the American Civil War, it was rewritten, emerging in a form that became known as Taps.

The man credited with creating Taps was General Daniel Butterfield of the Union Army. 'I could sound calls on the bugle as a necessary part of military knowledge and instruction for an officer commanding a regiment,' he was later to recall. He was, though, unable to 'write a note of music', so when he became dissatisfied with the existing call, thinking it not 'as smooth, melodious and musical as it should be', he was obliged to make changes by ear and have them written down by someone else. The new call was first sounded by his brigade bugler, Oliver Norton, and made an immediate impact. 'The music was beautiful on that still summer night, and was heard far beyond the limits of our brigade,' remembered Norton. 'The next day I was visited by several buglers from neighbouring brigades, asking for copies of the music, which I gladly furnished.' Taps swiftly replaced the existing Tattoo throughout the Union Army and even, perhaps, in the opposing Confederate ranks as well.

Like the Last Post, it soon became more than a literal reference to the end of the day, acquiring a symbolic meaning to signify the end of life. The US Army's *Infantry Drill Regulations* in 1891 made its use mandatory in military funerals, though this merely recognised a practice that was already established.

Indeed the first claimed use of Taps at the burial of a soldier comes from July 1862, the same month that it had been written. There was, in this instance, no prompting by the name of the piece, and it seems more likely that its rapid adoption as a lament stemmed instead from the haunting beauty of the call when first heard in the aftermath of battle on a warm Virginia night. It is possible that the use of Taps at funerals was adapted from the British use of the Last Post, but there is no evidence of such an influence. The militaries of the two countries may have come upon the metaphorical use of their respective calls within just a few years of each other, but most likely they did so independently. It was, perhaps, simply an idea whose time had come.

The development was not matched elsewhere, however. The Prussian army had its own version of Tattoo, known as the Zapfenstreich (a word with similar roots, meaning 'tap strike'), which dated back to the sixteenth century and had evolved separately. Originally just a trumpet call, it became customary in the early nineteenth century to follow it, where there was a band available, with a hymn, so that the day ended on a religious note. 'First of all, a roll on the drum calls your attention, then the post is magnificently played, and lastly the evening hymn,' wrote the *Daily Telegraph*'s correspondent, stationed with a German force camped out in the woods during the Franco-Prussian War in 1870. 'I shall certainly not easily forget the impression made upon me as I listened to the beautiful strains of holy music, and gazed upon the beautiful forest, lit up by the light of ten thousand bivouac fires, surrounded by the soldiers.'

From this came the modern German and Austrian practice of the Große Zapfenstreich, a torchlight ceremony of such solemn and sacred standing that its use is reserved for state occasions and for honouring the holders of the highest civil and military offices. The equivalent to the Last Post at German military funerals, however, derived from an entirely different source: the song 'Ich hatt' einen Kameraden' ('I Had a Comrade'), an 1825 setting by Friedrich Silcher of an earlier poem by Ludwig Uhland.

Although the funereal function of Taps and the Last Post had emerged almost simultaneously on both sides of the Atlantic, there was a subsequent parting of the ways, perhaps in consequence of the different military cultures of the two countries. There was no British equivalent to those US regulations of 1891 that instituted the playing of Taps at soldiers' funerals, and which was to lead to every veteran being entitled to a burial with full military honours. In Britain there was simply no official recognition at all of the Last Post in this context. Instead, the custom, which had started out in piecemeal fashion, continued to grow in the same manner.

The call was sounded at the funerals of some of the great commanders — at the interments of the Duke of Cambridge in 1904 and of Viscount Wolseley in 1913 — but it also had a separate, semi-official existence. It was not, for example, played at the funeral of Queen Victoria, though it was heard at various memorial services to her across the country, in places both grand and humble, from Chester Cathedral to Didsbury Parish Church. Mostly it was reserved for servicemen, but not simply for those killed on active duty: a soldier named Scattergood who died in the terrible fire at the Theatre Royal, Exeter, in 1887 was also buried to the accompaniment of the Last Post.

With time, as the practice became better known, it started to spread beyond the ranks of the military to include the likes of John Brown Paton, a noted theologian who had never served in uniform, but whose funeral in 1911 ended with the call being sounded by buglers from the Boys' Brigade. Similarly, the following year saw the laying to rest of Wallace Hartley, the bandmaster who had died in the sinking of the *Titanic*, an event that drew huge crowds of over thirty thousand to Colne, Lancashire. 'Flags were at half-mast on the Town Hall and all public buildings, and every house in the town had its blinds drawn,' it was reported. 'The ceremony, which was of a very affecting character, terminated with the Last Post, sounded by a large number of bugler scouts.'

Hartley's family and friends had at least the consolation that his body was returned for burial. Many others lost at sea were never recovered. In 1906 a funeral service was held on board HMS *Pegasus* for a sailor named Moses Bunker who had drowned in the harbour at Wellington, New Zealand. As three volleys were fired, the Last Post was sounded and white chrysanthemums were scattered on the waves. It marked the dawn of a new tradition, for this was the first time the Royal Navy had ever conducted a full funeral for a man lost overboard when the body could not be retrieved. With the precedent set, future such services would include those conducted over the last resting-places of the early submarines HMS *C11*, which sank near Cromer, Norfolk, in 1909, and HMS *A7*, similarly lost in Whitsand Bay, Cornwall, early in 1914.

The rise and spread of the Last Post as a funeral anthem coincided with a steady improvement in the public image of the soldier. Shortly after the Crimean War, Lord Panmure, secretary of state for war, had spoken out in praise of how army life had been transformed from a generation earlier. 'If you go into any of our barrack yards you will find them now with schools of instruction, with reading-rooms for non-commissioned officers and soldiers, with places for recreation and exercise, and you will find them leading a life of Christian

The sight of the bugle boy in a scarlet tunic became one of the most celebrated images of the British Army in the late nineteenth century

usefulness,' he enthused. And, he added, 'the army at this time may present its ranks to the farmer and shopkeeper and manufacturer as being a fit profession for their children, without their leaving that army in the course of a few years debased and degraded as they would have done in former times.'

If this was jumping the gun a little, there were certainly moves afoot to modernise the Army, to cast off the old image of an institution run by officers who had purchased their commissions, and to create something resembling professionalism. One of Panmure's successors, the Liberal Edward Cardwell, who served as war secretary from 1868 to 1874, introduced a wave of reforms to military life that reduced the minimum period of service and ended flogging. The process culminated in 1881 with the reorganisation of the regimental structure in the infantry: the old system of numbering regiments was abandoned in favour of geographical associations, so that the 22nd Foot, for example, became the Cheshire Regiment, and the 24th Foot became the South Wales Borderers. The new allegiances with local recruitment areas began to build bridges between military and civilian life.

So too did the music of the Army. Military bands had once been essentially a private affair. Financed directly by the officers of a regiment, primarily for the purpose of enlivening evenings in the mess, they had ventured out in public only to encourage enlistment; now they increasingly came under the control of the War Office and found a new role as providers of public entertainment. In the second half of the nineteenth century, with the Empire at its peak, and with a prolonged interlude of peace, the sight of bandsmen in scarlet tunics became the most familiar face of the Army in Britain. Regimental bands were capable of attracting crowds of fifty, even a hundred, thousand when playing in the parks of London, Manchester and the other great cities, and their role as public relations ambassadors was invaluable in the gradual re-evaluation of the armed forces.

Nonetheless, old attitudes survived in many quarters, and recruitment into the army remained largely the preserve of those families with a tradition of soldiering. Despite Panmure's words, many outside remained sceptical of the virtues of a military career. Laurie Dunn, who was later to become a bandmaster, recalled that his father had to run away to join the ranks in the 1880s because he wouldn't have got his parents' consent: 'they hated the Army — that was the general feeling in those days.'

Conversely, there was too, even after W.H. Russell's revelations of the realities of military life, a romantic perception of conflict, a belief that battle was, above all, a matter of glory and gallantry. The heroism of Tennyson's 'Charge of the Light Brigade' meant more than the blundering. Chivalry, it was assumed by the popular writers of the time, remained a noble ideal even in Victorian Britain. 'Women suffer most from wars, no doubt,' observed a character in one of G.A. Henty's adventure novels (Henty himself had been a war correspondent in the Crimea); 'yet they are more stirred by deeds of valour and chivalry than are we men; they are ever ready to bestow their love upon those who have won honour and glory in war, even though the next battle may leave them widows.'

And since Britain fought its battles abroad and tended to emerge on the side of the victors, the appetite at home for foreign adventures remained undiminished. When there was further trouble between Russia and the Ottoman Empire in 1878, the music hall star G.H. MacDermott scored his greatest hit with 'MacDermott's War Song', a piece whose rousing chorus introduced the word 'jingoism' into the language:

We don't want to fight, but by jingo if we do,
We've got the ships, we've got the men, and got the money
too!

As Rudyard Kipling once wrote: 'The people enjoyed all the glory of war with none of the risks.'

It was Kipling who best captured Britain's contradictory attitudes towards the army with his hugely popular *Barrack-Room Ballads* (1892), most famously in the poem 'Tommy', which depicted the soldier as being unwanted in peacetime, turned away from theatres and pubs ('We serve no redcoats here'), but cheered and idolised 'when the guns begin to shoot'. Kipling insisted that soldiers weren't merely the drunken ruffians of popular prejudice, but, unlike those earlier poets who had written of 'The Soldier's Funeral', he had no sentimental image of them as being somehow a gallant breed apart:

We aren't no thin red 'eroes, nor we aren't no blackguards
too.
But single men in barricks, most remarkable like you;
An' if sometimes our conduck isn't all your fancy paints,
Why single men in barricks don't grow into plaster saints.

Soon after that poem's publication, following decades of relative peace in the Empire, tensions with the Boer settlers in South Africa erupted into the Second Boer War. There had been minor colonial conflicts in the years since the Crimean campaign, but this was immediately seen as something much more serious and exciting; the Boers were Christian, white and European – a worthy foe – and the outbreak of war in October 1899 was greeted with great enthusiasm in Britain. Early on, some Liberal politicians, most notably John Morley, courted unpopularity by calling for 'determined opposition to the jingoism – there is no better word for it – which has undoubtedly been making its way amongst all classes in the country', but they were in a very definite minority. So widespread was the fervour that even the era's best-loved fictional anti-hero, E.W. Hornung's gentleman thief A.J. Raffles, sought redemption for his sins in South Africa. 'Old schoolfellows had fallen, and I know Raffles envied them,' wrote his chronicler; 'he spoke so wistfully of such an end.' And in June 1900, the old rogue died a hero's death on the veldt.

Such celebrations of the nobility of war did not go unchallenged as the conflict continued until May 1902, the full might of the Empire seemingly unable to quash the irregular forces of Boer farmers. At home there was political disquiet about the tactics being employed against non-combatants, and in Europe little support was to be found, with one Austrian newspaper reaching for a familiar phrase: 'If ever a war could be called a people's war, this is indeed one,' it opined; 'but it is a hopeless struggle.' This time the reference was not to the British people.

The Boer War was the first major conflict since the Last Post had become a common feature of military funerals, and the piece was played with depressing regularity throughout the hostilities, for there were as many fatalities in South Africa as there had been in the Crimea. (Again, the majority of deaths were the result of disease rather than wounds.) Where there was no opportunity to sound it at the time, it was performed later as a retrospective rite. Following the relief of Mafeking in May 1900, after a siege lasting over seven months, a day of thanksgiving was held in the town; this included a service at the cemetery where so many had been hurriedly buried, without due ceremony, under cover of night. 'We have been unable to fire a volley over the graves of our killed, being fearful of drawing the fire of the enemy's guns,' explained Colonel Robert Baden-Powell, the hero of the siege. Those omissions were now rectified and full honours were accorded to the dead; 'surely they lived again when, in their honour and to their memory, the bugles rang out the Last Post,' reflected George Tighe, a civilian who had served in the Town Guard. The high feeling stirred by the service was noted in the reports: 'After sounding the Last Post, the garrison attempted to sing the national anthem, but could hardly be heard, as the men choked with emotion.'

That use of the call not simply at a funeral but at a commemoration service was a significant shift in the evolution of the Last Post, and it was replicated at home in the aftermath of the South African campaign. The idea of the war memorial, born in the wake of the Crimea campaign, matured with the Boer War. Over the next few years, more than six hundred monuments were unveiled across the country, listing the dead of regiments, of schools, of towns and cities. So frequent were the unveilings that the dedication of the memorial to the Coldstream Guards in St Paul's Cathedral was simply headlined in one paper: ANOTHER WAR MEMORIAL.

Some of these monuments were not confined to South Africa, but yoked in other campaigns; such as the memorial in Wrexham for members of the Royal Welch Fusiliers 'who have recently fallen on active service in South Africa and China'. Some listed non-combatants alongside the soldiers, particularly members of the St John Ambulance Brigade. Some were simple stone tablets, others were granite obelisks and, on top of Coombe Hill, Buckinghamshire, some 850 feet above sea level and overlooking the prime minister's country house, Chequers, there stood perhaps the most impressive of all, listing the names of 148 men from the county who had died. This was what they all had in common: the idea of recording names, which had now become accepted as standard practice. It was not generals, but soldiers, who were being honoured.

The other thing they all had in common was that the unveiling was invariably accompanied by the sounding of the Last Post, now inextricably entwined in the public mind with the war dead and with memory. The call was becoming a symbolic link between the civilian and the soldier, bringing together their two worlds in a way that had seldom been seen before.

The phrase itself had entered popular consciousness and was increasingly used beyond the confines of the call itself. In 1903 Mildred G. Dooner published a book whose subtitle spelt out its contents: *A Roll Call of All Officers (Naval, Military or Colonial) Who Gave Their Lives for Their Queen, King and Country in the South African War 1899–1902*. Its main title was, almost inevitably by this stage, *The Last Post*. As she wrote in her Preface: 'The Last Post has sounded over the graves of those who sleep on the South African veldt and kopje, and this book, written in their memory, is only an echo of that bugle call; an epitaph to their bravery and heroism.'

Even as the conflict was at its height, the Boer War also inspired the poet W.E. Henley to write 'The Last Post', a piece which, if it never quite acquired the status of his best-known works 'Invictus' and 'Pro Rege Nostro', nonetheless briefly caught the imagination of the public when published in his collection *For England's Sake: Verses and Songs in Time of War* (1900). Unlike the spate of 'The Soldier's Funeral' poems some eighty years earlier, this emphasised patriotism rather than pathos, with its lament for, and celebration of, those

who had died; its theme was not individual loss but sacrifice
for the greater imperial good:

> So to the Maker of homes, to the Giver of bread,
> For whose dear sake their triumphing souls they shed,
> Blow, you bugles of England, blow,
> Though you break the heart of her beaten foe,
> Glory and praise to the everlasting Mother,
> Glory and peace to her lovely and faithful dead!

Some, even at the time, felt the tone a little ill-judged – the
Spectator concluded it was 'fine but somewhat thrasonical' – but
the poem proved sufficiently popular that within a couple of
months it had been set to music by Charles Villiers Stanford,
the most distinguished Irish musician of his day. Stanford's
Last Post, op. 75, was first performed at Buckingham Palace in
June 1900, with its public debut coming at the Hereford
Festival that September. A piece for chorus and orchestra, it
was, wrote the composer's biographer, a 'simple but effective
work', opening with massed trumpets playing the Last Post and
ending with the call repeated on a solo bugle, 'where Stanford
asks the player to begin his call independently of the orchestra's
tempo at a distance from or behind the platform'. This was
how it was staged at Hereford to great acclaim: 'The effect of
the bugle call was very much enhanced by the fact that it was
played by an extra trumpet in the Lady Chapel at the far end of
the Cathedral.' The performance was reported across the
world, with a local paper in Adelaide saying that the piece
'scored an immediate success and should soon become popular
in Australasia for patriotic celebrations'.

As the war progressed, there were further performances of
Last Post, and then, though there were to be occasional revivals,

it began to fade from the repertoire of choral societies. It did, however, represent the first significant use of the bugle in a work by a serious composer. Elevated by the solemn associations built up around the Last Post, Stanford's piece transported the call from the parade ground to the concert hall, a symbol of its embrace by civilian society.

Meanwhile, as thoughts of the conflict were being kept alive by the memorials, Britain resumed a peacetime existence that was not destined to last. In 1904 Edward Stanley, a Conservative MP who had himself served in the Boer War, unveiled a plaque at Abbott Street School, Manchester, for five old boys who had died in South Africa, the first time such a monument had been raised in an elementary school. He took the opportunity to argue that memorials were rather wasted in churches, where they 'were seen perhaps only once a week, and then only by people who already appreciated the duties and obligations upon them'. Those who would really benefit from being reminded of the virtue of national sacrifice, he suggested, were the young, for whom 'there might come a moment – all hoped it would be long postponed – when the country would have to call on them for service as it had called upon their fathers in the past'.

Despite his hopes, it transpired that the moment was not long postponed at all, for the country was less than a decade from the outbreak of the First World War. During that conflict Lord Stanley, now the 17th Earl of Derby, was promoted to become secretary of state for war, whilst every one of the schoolboys who heard him speak that day had become eligible for service.

Chapter Three

CHARGE

Now, who are ye that cross the sea
To the bugles' breaking key?
Mother, we are your eldest born
That claim to follow the sounding horn.
Carry on! Carry on!
For England must be free.

Maurice Hewlett
'The Bugles' (1915)

That there top note of the Last Post on the bugle doesn't 'arf sound proper,' reflected a cockney soldier. 'But if the bugler's 'ad a drop o' somethin' warm on the way to the cemetery, that there top note always reminds him of a 'iccup. An' if 'e 'iccups over me, I shall wanter spit in 'is eye, blimey if I won't.'

The chance of such an eventuality was very real. The year was 1917, and the speaker was lying in a British Army hospital in France, where his wounds were judged to be so serious that he had been put on the danger list. 'In spite of considerable pain, he poked fun at the prospect of his own imminent demise,' it was reported. 'He would talk; and he would talk about undertakers, post-mortems, epitaphs and the details of a military funeral.'

There was, perhaps, little else to talk of, for death was omnipresent. Field hospitals were located near improvised and newly designated cemeteries, for reasons that were obvious in logistical, if not psychological terms, and the proximity can have done little to lift the spirits of the injured and dying. Those who succumbed to their wounds, and those whose lifeless bodies could be recovered from the battlefield, were accorded full military funerals. Even in a small cemetery, therefore, the sound of the Last Post might be heard twenty, thirty, forty times a day by those who remained, reminding them again and again of their possible fate, as they lay, clinging to hopes of recovery or repatriation.

Britain had declared war on Germany on the 4th of August 1914, and popular sentiment, prepared by many years of anti-German messages in newspapers and popular magazines, was strongly in support of the coming confrontation; it was widely believed that this would be a short, salutary lesson to a country that seemed to think it could challenge the supremacy of the British Empire. The eagerness for battle was sufficiently removed from reality that senior politicians attempted to dampen down the more unrealistic expectations, with Lord Curzon, the former Viceroy of India, saying that he was 'perfectly shocked when he read in the papers of people talking about the war being over by Christmas', since he was convinced that 'more than one Christmas would pass before our soldiers returned'. (The same popular attitude was also evident in Germany, from where it was reported that 'everybody thought the Germans would have a kind of picnic, and that all would be over by Christmas'.)

Although plans for a British Expeditionary Force had long been in place, it was immediately recognised that the regular army would need a massive infusion of new men to sustain what was likely to be a protracted conflict. Whilst these new troops were being recruited and trained, however, the first forces to be sent to France were comprised of the professional soldiers who were already enlisted. By Christmas 1914, this army had been almost destroyed, and the scale of the enterprise was becoming horribly apparent. The first battle of Ypres, a month-long encounter that ended in November that year, resulted in fifty-six thousand British casualties, more than double the number of British soldiers who had taken the field at Waterloo a century earlier. This, it was becoming rapidly apparent, was a war unlike anything Britain had previously encountered, and the volunteer army that was being raised at home by Lord Kitchener was called upon sooner than expected to fill the gaps. There was, however, no shortage of personnel at this stage; a quarter of a million men had signed up in the first month of hostilities. That was to change as the conflict dragged on, bogged down in the stalemate of trench warfare.

As casualties increased, the numbers choosing to step forward as volunteers began to decline and, in January 1916, for the first time in British history, conscription was introduced, initially for all single men aged between eighteen and forty-one who were not in reserved occupations necessary for the war effort, and then for all such men, whether single or married. The mood at home was turning from passion to fatalism, a grim realisation that things had gone too far to turn back. And still the death toll mounted. During the first day of the battle of the Somme, on the 1st of July 1916, the British suffered some sixty thousand casualties, the greatest losses ever sustained by the British Army in a single day. The majority of them were volunteers. By the end of that battle, which was to last four and a half months, the number of dead and wounded on the two sides stood at over a million.

British recruitment poster from the First World War

It was in this terrible context that buglers were called upon to do their funereal duty. The practice was to bury the dead at the beginning and at the end of the day, at sunrise and sunset. Twice a day, a bugler would stand over grave after grave, playing the Last Post for a succession of strangers and comrades, knowing that any tremor in the lip would be heard. 'My third son spent about four years in France and played the Last Post over two thousand of our boys,' remembered Clara Graves of Brighouse, Yorkshire, after the war. 'He tells me how reverently they were laid to rest. He and a few friends spent all their spare time carving crosses and taking photographs of graves for the comfort of those at home.'

Many of these buglers were very young. Fletcher Clough of Burnley joined the East Lancashire Regiment at the outbreak of hostilities aged just fifteen, a bugle boy with dreams of heroism and glory. He promised to send his younger brother 'the helmet of the first German I kill', but instead he was dead within ten months, having witnessed horrors beyond his years. Boys of that age were not officially permitted at the front, but in the confusion of war it was often difficult to keep track. When two fifteen-year-old buglers were discovered in the firing line in the Dardanelles, reported Private Walter Brown of the Lancashire Fusiliers, they were immediately instructed to return to base, much to their displeasure: 'both cried very bitterly indeed at not being allowed to stop with us, and both were very indignant.'

Those who were of age had a dual role. They served as ordinary soldiers in the trenches, facing hardships, wounds and death in the same manner as other frontline troops. 'I think of you when I am standing on sentry duty in a trench four inches deep with water, watching to see if any of the Germans are coming towards us whilst all my chums sleep, and listening to the bullets whistling all over the place,' bugler H. Blower of Coventry wrote home to his family, concluding with impressive understatement: 'I would rather be in Coventry.' And behind the lines, their chief duty was that playing of the Last Post at funerals. In these circumstances, it would hardly be surprising if, given the opportunity, a bugler did have 'a drop o' somethin' warm' to revive his flagging spirits on yet another trip to the cemetery.

The relentless repetition of the ritual placed enormous strain too upon the other figure who was present at a soldier's funeral: the padre who was called upon to officiate at the burials. There was a mutual respect between these two men, the bugler and the padre, both serving in a non-combatant capacity in the midst of war. 'He always comes when we send for him,' reflected one bugler, on the role of the padre on the Western Front. 'In the middle of the night he'll come, and he goes down into the trenches without a revolver or anything, and he'll go on with the service when he is burying a man, with shots being fired all round him.'

One such was James Owen Hannay, an Irish clergyman who was later to recount his experiences under the pen name George A. Birmingham. 'Here are huge cemeteries, long lines of graves, where every morning some are laid to rest, with reverence indeed, but with scant measure of the ritual pomp with which men are wont to pay their final honour to the dead,' he wrote. 'Yet, standing above the lines of rude coffins, viewing the names and numbers pencilled on the lids, our hearts are lifted up. We know how great it is to lay down life for others. The final wailing notes of the Last Post speak our feeling: "Good night. Good-bye. See you again, soon."'

The same scene was to be encountered both near and far. In Malta there were some twenty hospitals filled with wounded and convalescent soldiers, many of whom were destined never to leave the island. 'All through the heat of the day, since the burials which took place at sunrise, workmen have been busily engaged building new graves – deep, stone-lined sepulchres, to be filled again by night,' wrote the Reverend Victor MacEchern, who served in Malta in 1915; 'and in the evening, when the sun is setting and the sky in the west is filled with glory, gun-carriages roll up, each bearing its broken warrior, with the Union Jack draped over the coffin and a khaki helmet resting over it.' Again it was the reiteration that could overwhelm the soul. 'It is the same music from the band each morning and each evening, followed by the three sharp volleys of honour and the solemn sounding of the Last Post, whose notes seem to linger in the air as if loth to die.'

For those stationed in Africa, too, there was little relief to be found. John Bruce Cairn of the King's African Rifles was in Lindi, in what had until recently been known as German East Africa (and is now Tanzania). On the 13th of January 1918 he recorded in his diary: 'There are a good many crocking it in the hospital over the road – an average of one European a day, which is very little of course compared with France, but it gets monotonous hearing the Last Post.'

It was a complaint that had often been voiced in the past, even before the Last Post became an integral part of the funeral service. 'The hospitals were full of sick and dying; and from dawn of day till set of sun the streets re-echoed to the melancholy sounds of the fife and drum playing the Dead March as the departed soldier was borne to his last home,' recalled a soldier who had served with the British Legion during the First Carlist War in the 1830s. 'The ladies in the balconies caught up the air and continued it on their pianos; the very bugles that sounded the Reveille and Advance had a lugubrious sound, as if blown by a man in his grave; at length the Dead March in Saul became the only piece of music current in Vitoria.'

In a different context, protests were heard too in Australia during the First World War, this time about the use of the Last Post at recruiting meetings. 'I have no doubt that this call is sounded in honour of our fallen heroes, but surely the mothers and wives of these men might be considered,' wrote an ex-soldier, whose brother had been killed in France, to the *Brisbane Courier*. 'No one who has not lost a member of their family can realise how very sad the Last Post is, and I have frequently seen mothers break down on hearing the call sounded at these meetings.' His argument was supported by another veteran: 'Having done my bit in the past, and witnessed many funerals, I can state that nothing on active service gave me the creeps but the shrill notes of the Last Post.' He had an alternative proposal that he felt might attract, rather than repel, new recruits: 'As an old hand at the sword, may I suggest some lively cavalry calls such as Reveille, Boots and Saddles and Turn Out in place of the Last Post.'

None, however, wished to change the order of service at a funeral. For over half a century now, the Last Post had been sounded over the graves of dead soldiers and it was almost unthinkable that it should not be heard. Indeed, so important a part of the ceremony had it become that it was considered appropriate to sound the call even when it was to mark the passing of a foe. In 1900 Commandant C.J. de Villiers had died of his wounds in a Bloemfontein hospital and, although he had been – from a British perspective – on the wrong side of the war in South Africa, his remains were buried with full military honours, at a service that featured a band of the Yorkshire Regiment and the drums of the Royal Warwicks, concluding with the Last Post.

Australian recruitment poster from the First World War

The same courtesy was accorded to enemy combatants during the First World War. The first British shots fired in the conflict were those on the 5th of August 1914 aimed at SS *Königin Luise*, a German steam ferry that had been pressed into military service and was found laying mines in the Thames Estuary. The ship was sunk off Harwich, though it had already done its deadly work; early the next morning, the light cruiser HMS *Amphion* became the first British naval loss when it struck one of the mines that had been laid. The bodies of eight sailors, four from each side, were retrieved from the two ships and were buried in a single service, their remains borne on 'a country wagon containing eight coffins, four covered by the Union Jack and four by the German ensign'. At the cemetery, 'three volleys were fired over their graves and a British bugle sounded the Last Post'. Nor was burial with military honours restricted to those killed in combat; the funeral was held in 1915 of a German prisoner shot dead while trying to escape from Leigh Camp in Lancashire: 'Fourteen German soldiers with six wreaths attended under an escort, and three volleys were fired and the Last Post sounded.'

Such even-handedness might not have been expected to last long during such protracted hostilities, but there is no evidence of any change in attitude on the part of either officialdom or the public as the months and years wore on. In September 1916, two years after the sinking of the *Königin Luise*, the *SL11* became the first German airship to be shot down over Britain. All fifteen members of its crew were killed and were buried in Potters Bar in a funeral attended by a hundred men of the Royal Flying Corps. 'There was no outburst of indignation such as would have pleased writers in some newspapers,' observed the *Manchester Guardian*, in a tone of liberal relief. 'The attitude of the large crowd, on the contrary, was quiet and reverent.'

Similar respect was sometimes reported from the other side. In 1916, during the long and bloody siege of Kut in Iraq, it was said of the Turkish forces that 'Even the enemy refrained from bombarding when the sad, haunting wail of the bugle sounded the Last Post, filling the air with its shrill notes, till it plaintively faded away over the strangely stilled desert.'

For the most part, though, the sounding of the call in Britain during the First World War signified not the deaths of foes but those of friends and family, whether as individuals or as a remorselessly growing army of the dead. In churches and cemeteries across the country, the Last Post was heard at services honouring the deceased. Some were humble gatherings of family and friends, others were great formal occasions; some were local affairs, others international ceremonies, reaching out to Britain's allies. In 1915 a service of thanksgiving was held at St Paul's for those who had died during the doomed Gallipoli campaign: 'the silver notes of the Last Post, sobbing and echoing through the aisles, conveyed a sense of an open graveside, and caused many women to sink to their seats and burst quietly into tears, while the National Anthem was sung like a sacred battle song.' The following year Bastille Day was celebrated with a Requiem Mass in Westminster Cathedral, attended by the prime minister and the French ambassador to London. 'The massed bands of the Brigade of Guards played funereal music and at the end rolled out La Marseillaise and the National Anthem,' read the reports, adding, as though it were necessary: 'The buglers sounded the Last Post.'

A piece of music that had once been largely confined to the armed forces became during the course of the First World War fully absorbed into national life and culture. The sheer numbers involved in the fighting, first as volunteers and then as conscripts, ensured that armed service was no longer the province of military families. For the first time since the Civil War two and a half centuries earlier, this was a conflict that touched everyone in the country; the parallel worlds of the soldier and the civilian had merged, and all were brought together in a way that had no precedent in Britain. Furthermore, because this war, unlike those in the Crimea and in South Africa, was being waged so close to home it was possible to repatriate large numbers of the wounded; many were subsequently to die at home, and their funerals ensured that the Last Post was seldom absent from everyday life.

And it was − in the public mind − the infantry version of the call that became familiar. If this truly were a people's war, involving millions of men and women on active service abroad, and millions of families at home, then it seemed somehow appropriate that it was the humble bugle and not the aristocratic cavalry trumpet that was to accompany the massive losses that had to be endured. The spirit of democracy was abroad and the Last Post formed a key part of its soundtrack.

There arose too, a century on from 'The Soldier's Funeral', a vein of poetry, both professional and amateur, that took the title of 'The Last Post'. Some examples, such as E.S. Cohn's contribution from 1915, were pieces of patriotic tub-thumping:

> The land that gave such heroes birth
> Has need of thousands more;
> Come forth, ye men, to prove your worth
> And guard the name they bore,
> The name of Englishman, the sign
> Of rule and sov'reignty benign.

Others focused on the experience of bereavement, including E. Coungeau's poem, also from 1915:

No mournful sound of muffled drum so lone
Disturbs our dreams, no more clash of spears,
But up to Heaven ascends a woman's moan
The bitter agony of unshed tears.

Simplest, and perhaps most effective of all, was an anonymous poem that was 'found in the pocket-book of the late Lieutenant Leo Butler, killed in France, on his belongings being returned to his parents in Hobart':

A long, long night of rest,
And then the morning bright,
Reveille with the Blest.
Lights out!
Good night!

But nowhere, beyond the battlefields themselves, did the Last Post ring out with quite such impact and significance as in Cape Town during the final months of the conflict. On the 12th of April 1918, Major Walter Brydon of the South African Heavy Artillery, who had already been thrice wounded and once hospitalised after a gas attack, was killed in action. He was acclaimed at home as a hero: 'It was one of the many ironies of the war that he never received the Victoria Cross,' reflected John Buchan, 'for he won it a dozen times.' Brydon's father was a city councillor in Cape Town, and wrote to the *Cape Times* suggesting that a daily period of silence be held in the city to remember those who had died and those who were still fighting in Europe. The mayor, Sir Harry Hands, whose own son had served alongside Brydon and been mortally wounded in the same battle, approved the idea, and on the 14th of May 1918 the first three-minute silence was held. Its start was heralded by the Noon Gun, which had been fired every day since 1806 from Signal Hill in the centre of the city; this was now immediately to be followed by a solo bugler playing the Last Post, and the silence to be ended with the sounding of Reveille.

The midday pause, its duration subsequently reduced by Hands to two minutes 'in order to better retain its hold on the people', was to be repeated every day in the city even beyond the cessation of hostilities, until the 17th of January 1919. It was an extraordinary phenomenon. Every single day for the best part of a year, life in Cape Town came to a halt in honour of a war being fought five thousand miles away.

The impact of that example would later be felt throughout the Empire, but at the time an equally extraordinary phenomenon was the lack of attention that the Cape Town silence attracted in the British press. Or perhaps it was simply that by this stage such an observance had been overtaken by greater events, with ripples that spread far beyond the British Empire. In April 1917 the United States of America entered the conflict on the side of the Allies opposing Germany, the first time that it had sent troops to fight in Europe. And in November that year the Bolsheviks led a communist revolution in Russia, taking the country out of the war.

The impact of that revolution, providing an inspiration for socialists throughout the world, in Britain, America and elsewhere, was not to be felt fully until after the cessation of hostilities. But clearly it didn't augur well for future stability in Europe. The appalling damage that had been visited upon Belgium and France, and the national humiliation that was to be experienced by Germany, were augmented by upheavals in Russia that many in authority feared would spread through the industrialised world.

The war itself took another year to resolve, but by summer 1918 it was clear that the Allies were gaining the upper hand and that an end was in sight. Finally, at five o'clock, French time, on the morning of the 11th of November 1918 an armistice was signed by Germany and the Allies. 'Eleven o'clock today, November 11, troops will stand fast on the positions reached at the hour named,' read the terse order that was sent out to British units. 'All military precautions will be preserved, and there will be no communication with the enemy.'

In many places the end was not quite as dramatic as it might have been. For the last couple of days, as peace became inevitable, the precise line of the front had been blurred by uprooted French and Belgian civilians as they began to make their way homewards, and there was consequently no sudden silence, no hush that descended where moments before there had been artillery bombardments and rifle fire. Elsewhere it was reported that 'up to the moment that the armistice began, the artillery and machine-guns on both sides have been busily at work as though there was no thought of hostilities coming to an end'.

Meanwhile, in towns just behind the front lines, bugles sounded the Cease Fire and bands played the national anthems of France, Belgium and the United Kingdom, followed in some instances by 'It's a Long Way to Tipperary', a music-hall song that had been adopted by the troops and 'which the peasantry seem to imagine is our national anthem, to judge by the respect with which they hearkened to the strains'. Right across the front, the emotion seemed to be one of weary, cautious relief rather than of wild celebration. 'It's over, mate,' a lorry driver was reported to have shouted out to a passing gunner. 'Too good to be true,' the artilleryman replied. 'I'll wake up presently.'

Back home, on the other hand, the note was one of pure, unadulterated jubilation. Workers all over the country in mills and mines and, most poignantly, in munitions factories downed tools and staged an unofficial half-day holiday that in most cases extended to the following day as well. Those in rural areas who had access to transport headed for the nearest town, and in every village and city street there were crowds celebrating the end of four years of suffering. There had never been a better opportunity for a party, nor one that was embraced with such joyous enthusiasm.

The imminent announcement of the armistice was expected, of course, and the means of its broadcast were appropriate to the circumstances. In October 1917 the government had decreed that the end of an air raid should be signalled not by whistles but by bugles sounding the All Clear. That function had been allocated to adolescent boys, wearing red tunics and mounted on bicycles. Now they were once more in evidence; in the major cities of England, the maroons that had once warned of the imminence of enemy bombs were fired again, followed immediately by the appearance on the streets of these 'chubby little angels of goodwill'. 'In the West End,' wrote a London-based reporter for *The Times*, 'they say a policeman held the bugle: but here it was a red-headed, russet-faced boy on a bicycle. He blew as if he had resolved on doing nothing else for the term of his natural life.'

His equivalent on the front lines in France was less fresh-faced, less ebullient. Sydney Golledge of Bath had joined the Somerset Light Infantry as a bugler in 1914 and was still with the regiment in 1918, returning to the front from a spell of home leave on the morning of the 11th of November, just in time to sound the Cease Fire. After four years of active service, he was now nineteen years old.

Graves at Passchendaele Ridge, 1918

Chapter Four

CEASE FIRING

When with the morrow's dawn the bugle blew,
For the first time it summoned you in vain,
The Last Post does not sound for such as you,
But God's Reveille wakens you again.

Anonymous
'Missing' (1917)

The 11th of November 1918 fell on a Monday, and for the rest of that week there were wild celebrations all over the country. If the first need was to be out on the streets, sharing in the public merriment, the second was to find a musical expression of the exultation. Brass bands from the Salvation Army, who 'mingled patriotic airs with their mission hymns', were joined by ensembles of bugles and drums, sometimes composed of Boy Scouts, sometimes of amateurs with more enthusiasm than ability. 'In almost every main street at any time during the evening one could see such a band, with its flag-waving leader and its long straggling tail of men and girls linking arms across the street,' it was reported from Manchester. In Bristol, 'one of these peregrinating orchestras rejoiced in a bugle and a drum; biscuit boxes supplied the instruments for the rest of the band,' while in Battle, 'a band marched up and down the main street, which, if not of the most musical description, did its best and was at least attractive'.

Most of the festivities were good natured, with perhaps just a hint of gleeful gloating: in Sittingbourne on the Tuesday night an effigy of the Kaiser was given a mock funeral, complete with the Last Post, 'followed by terrific cheering', and the next night a likeness of the German crown prince was burnt in Coventry, again to the accompaniment of the Last Post 'and the crowd cheering lustily'. Every night that week, huge crowds thronged the streets and parks of London, rejoicing in the peace. Given the numbers killed over the previous four years, not everyone approved of the incessant partying, but the feelings of relief and of survival could not be contained. Even amongst the bereaved, the occasion was marked; on the morning of Armistice Day, a family in Derby received news that their son had been killed, yet still they hung a flag out of their window.

The crowds in the capital reached their peak on the Saturday, when the numbers grew so great that bus routes had hurriedly to be amended so as to avoid the now impassable major thoroughfares in the West End. When the evening came, bonfires were lit and fireworks set off, and the multitude, equipped with whistles and rattles to accompany the music provided by 'mixed but vigorous bands', grew so great and unruly that the authorities began to be concerned. 'It is undesirable that the cessation of hostilities should be celebrated in such a manner as to cause disorder and damage in the metropolis,' warned the Commissioner of the Metropolitan Police, though in truth he knew his force was powerless to stop the party. In any event, the largest numbers were to be found in Hyde Park where the ministry of munitions was staging an official firework display, the first time since the commencement of hostilities that such a spectacle had been seen in London. It may not have lived up to the standards of pre-war displays – it had been a long time since gunpowder had been spared for the making of fireworks — but that was never going to dampen the enthusiasm of the masses.

The following Saturday, Hyde Park was again the centre of attention, though this time the event had a more sober aspect, for this was a gathering of men wearing the silver badge awarded — for 'services rendered' — to those who had been given an honourable discharge from the armed forces as a result of their wounds. Between fifteen and twenty-five thousand men paraded in the presence of the King, Queen and Prince of Wales, watched by many thousands of civilian and military well-wishers.

The greatest reception was given to the men from St Dunstan's hostel for blind ex-servicemen, marching 'eight abreast with locked arms', each rank having at its centre a woman from the Voluntary Aid Detachment, guiding them by the arm. 'Are we downhearted?' they cried, and were answered with a resounding 'No!' from the crowd. 'Have we won?' they called again, and were met with an even louder cheer. At their head was Captain Beachcroft Towse, formerly of the Gordon Highlanders, whose heroism during the Boer War had won him the Victoria Cross and cost him his sight. 'Many eyes in the crowd grew dim,' it was reported, 'as he gave the "Eyes left" when his sightless company passed the King.'

The order and the formality of the parade did not last, however, for — even as the procession was making its slow progress around the park — impatience overtook those who were still awaiting their turn, and there came from the crowd of silver-badged men a great rush towards the royal party. 'Thousands of men surged forward, hundreds of hands shot out to grasp the King's hand,' reported A.E. Stanley, secretary of the Cheltenham branch of the National Federation of Discharged and Demobilised Soldiers and Sailors. 'Police and

Life Guards were powerless. The King was nearly lifted off his horse, the men wanting to chair him. He laughed very heartily, but was visibly moved at this unexpected outburst.' In the crush, the Prince of Wales and his horse became separated from the others, leaving the Prince with just two policemen to escort him, while army officers clambered onto the steps of the carriage containing the Queen to ensure her safety. Mounted police tried to push the throngs back, but the King shouted at them: 'For God's sake, go away. Don't you see the men are enjoying themselves.' It was, reported *The Times*, 'a loyal frenzy'.

Despite the life-changing injuries and disabilities on display – and the occasional moment of panic – it was a joyous occasion that brought together the monarch and his subjects in a moment of celebration. The previous weekend, a group of ex-servicemen had marched through the London streets bearing a banner that read: 'We want no Bolshevist government', and the silver badge parade seemed to reinforce that sentiment. The British working class, it appeared, could be relied upon to resist the siren song of revolution emanating from Russia, where the Tsar had first been overthrown and then, in July 1918, shot, along with his family. 'If a counterblast were sought to a republican movement in this country,' observed one paper, then surely this was it: 'Father and son relished the experience of such unconventional homage, and laughed heartily with their good-natured admirers.'

That, at least, was the official version of events. Other accounts suggested a very different atmosphere, with one later version saying that the surge forward had been prompted by angry cries of 'Where *is* this land fit for heroes?' This detail was probably an embellishment, for the speech in which that slogan was first aired – 'What is our task? To make Britain a fit country for heroes to live in' – had not yet been reported;

it was being made that very same day in Wolverhampton by David Lloyd George, as he launched the government's general election campaign. Nonetheless, the Prince of Wales was said to have detected early on in the parade 'a sullen unresponsiveness', and to have noted later: 'It dawned on me that the country was discontented and disillusioned.'

If there was such a mood, it was not yet widely expressed, though that would come. For now the sweet scent of victory still filled the land, and the election, held on the 14th of December 1918, saw sweeping gains for the Conservative Party in a coalition headed by Lloyd George of the Liberals, who was being billed in the *Daily Mirror* as 'The man who won the war, and the man who gave women the vote.' (The Representation of the People Act, earlier that year, had doubled the size of the electorate to include women over the age of thirty and all men over twenty-one.) Sinn Féin, fielding candidates for the first time in a general election, emerged with the third largest number of MPs, though the party's representatives refused to take their seats in Westminster, whilst the Labour Party tripled its share of the vote but still only secured fifty-seven MPs; various fringe socialist parties registered a negligible vote between them. The following month Sinn Féin unilaterally set up its own government in Dublin, and declared Ireland's independence. But on the mainland, little appetite for revolution was discernible.

Meanwhile the commemorations and celebrations continued; with the signing of the Treaty of Versailles in June 1919, they reached what was clearly intended to be a climax the following month, with twin parades in Paris and in London, the first on a Monday, the second on the following Saturday.

The Paris parade was said to have been a 'majestic and moving spectacle', inspiring feelings of solemn reverence:

'perhaps even Frenchmen did not know till then of what emotions they were capable.' According to *The Times*, 'The dominant note of it all is gratitude to the troops themselves, rather than to their leaders,' though the leaders were hardly forgotten: at the head of the British contingent of bands and servicemen marched the recently ennobled Field Marshal Douglas Haig, accompanied by no fewer than eighteen generals.

The procession had been heralded by the construction of a monument 'in the form of a truncated pyramid, fifty-five feet high, surmounted by an immense urn', that was placed under the Arc de Triomphe until the night before the parade. This was then moved to one side, to allow troops to march through the Arc, though it remained at the centre of attention: 'Sunlight glinting upon its four gilded figures of victory, with the forest of palms placed at its foot, make it one of the most impressive features of all the great pageant.'

Britain too required a monument, a physical focus for its parade on the 19th of July, now dubbed Peace Day. Just two weeks before the day itself, Lloyd George summoned the country's greatest architect, Sir Edwin Lutyens, and asked him to design 'a point of homage to stand as a symbol of remembrance worthy of an Empire mourning for its million dead'. He was thinking, he said, of a catafalque, but Lutyens corrected him: 'not a catafalque but a cenotaph'.

The term itself, a Greek word meaning 'empty tomb', was little known in Britain and even the pronunciation was uncertain; some classics teachers insisted that it should be pronounced 'Keenotaph', though 'Sennataph' won the day. Inevitably it carried echoes of the empty tomb at the heart of the Christian Resurrection, though the memorial was to bear no religious inscriptions, in deference to the multiple faiths of the Empire: to the Jews, Hindus, Muslims and others who had died in the war. The lack of any overt reference that might tie the monument to a specific religion also chimed with Lutyens's own feelings. 'All religions have some truth in them,' he had written to his wife in 1914, 'and all should be held in reverence.'

Instead it was created as a symbol of human loss, making no attempt to capture the scale of the dead, but merely pointing to an absence. And it did so in a form that immediately captured the hearts of the British public. Few were able to explain what it was that so enthralled them about this wooden structure, covered in plaster to resemble marble, this 'simple classical cenotaph, tall and narrow and white', but the answer probably lay in the elegant curves of the piece. 'The Cenotaph contains no vertical or horizontal lines,' explained Lutyens's biographer, Christopher Hussey. 'The four corners if produced upwards, would meet at a point about 1,000 feet above; all the horizontal lines are radials of circles from a common centre at 900 feet below ground.' It evoked the image of a segment cut from a monument too vast in size to exist in physical form, a slice of eternity. The subtlety of the lines, said Lutyens, gave it 'a life that cannot pertain to rectangular blocks of stone'.

On the morning of Peace Day, with the Cenotaph now in place in the middle of Whitehall, the Last Post was sounded as four guardsmen took up their positions on the corners of the structure, with bowed heads and arms reversed.

And then came the parade, one of the largest ever staged in Britain. Four hours it took for the various contingents to march past, representatives not merely of the Empire, and of France and the USA, but also of all the other Allies: troops from Belgium, China, Czechoslovakia, Greece, Italy, Japan, Poland, Portugal, Romania, Serbia and Siam, led by generals and staff officers in each instance. At every point on the six-mile route, the streets were densely packed on both sides with people, up to a quarter of a mile deep. 'This time there were no thin places in the crowd as at the Coronation,' it was noted, and indeed the numbers were claimed to have exceeded those seen at George V's Coronation or even at the Diamond Jubilee celebrations of his grandmother, Queen Victoria. So crowded was it that hundreds of thousands simply gave up and made their way instead to Hyde Park, where one would-be spectator concluded that, however fine the procession might be, 'this seems finer still, this gathering together of our people, this utterly mutual celebration of a great achievement'.

On the parade, it was reported that the crowd 'shouted themselves hoarse with delight when the victorious commanders passed', the biggest cheers coming for Marshal Foch, Admiral Beatty and Field Marshal Haig. The last of these was looking pale and frail; he had caught a chill but had decided to appear, heedless of his doctor's advice: 'Had he not done so the universal disappointment would have been very deep,' noted the press. Even Lord Kitchener of Khartoum, whose image on a recruitment advertisement was to become perhaps the most famous poster in history, was present in spirit; he had died in 1916, but his image adorned the route of the procession, and on the Strand there was a large display, 'the centre of which is a portrait of Kitchener with the legend: The man we must not forget'.

The mood was festive. 'It was a merry scene,' it was observed, 'a pardonably light-hearted crowd.' The one exception on the entire route, in the whole of central London, was at the Cenotaph itself. As the procession split into two columns, passing either side of the monument with reversed arms, a 'stillness that was almost felt took possession of the vast multitude, and the bands ceased playing. The dead were being honoured.' Already the Cenotaph was being talked of as 'this sacred point', and long after the parade had finished, there was still a steady stream of people making their way towards it, pausing for a few moments in silent contemplation, and then moving on. It was an oasis of reverence in a world of joy.

That evening saw the revelry start in earnest in the central London parks, most especially in Hyde Park where a diverse programme of entertainment had been laid on, ranging from a ten thousand-strong Imperial Choir of Peace, accompanied by the massed bands of the Brigade of Guards, all the way to a selection of 'Old English dances performed by the Misses Chaplin'. During the course of the evening, heavy rain set in, sending crowds scurrying for the refreshment tents, where queues of those seeking admission stretched back, ten abreast, for a mile. Spirits were undampened, however, and this time the fireworks display was truly impressive, a spectacle that seemed to evoke the night sky of the Western Front, transforming the horrors into a festive carnival: 'Rockets went up with the shock of heavy artillery, and high in the air exploded into great bursts of stars, with a roar like rapid musketry fire, and the great sea of human faces looked pallid in the white light.'

The only sour note in Hyde Park came after midnight, at a time when the celebrations were all supposed to have come to an end. The multitude showed no sign of wanting to go home, and instead built huge bonfires, throwing all the chairs that could be found into the conflagration; when police officers tried to rescue the furniture from the flames, 'the crowd merely laughed at their efforts, and whenever opportunity presented itself, more chairs were thrown'. Despite the best efforts of the police to stop the merry-making, the dancing and singing went on until three o'clock in the morning, the party punctuated by repeated skirmishes between revellers and the forces of law and order, clashes that were later blamed on 'the work of organised gangs of roughs who had come into the Park bent on mischief'.

There were similar festivities across the Empire, particularly in Canada, where Peace Day was declared a national holiday, and in Australia. Again, amidst the celebrations, there were pauses of still, silent remembrance, as in the parade at Melbourne: 'It was a solemn moment when the procession halted and the buglers of each regiment in turn sounded the Last Post.'

At the heart of that spirit of remembrance, it was now felt, was the Cenotaph in Whitehall. If the plaintive spirituality of the Last Post could ever be captured in physical form, then this was it, and on the Monday following Peace Day, *The Times* was not alone in suggesting that it become an enduring part of the Empire's capital: 'Sir Edwin Lutyens's design is so grave, suave and beautiful that one might well wish it were indeed of stone and permanent.' The 'truncated pyramid' in Paris, also known as a cenotaph, had been removed and discarded, destroyed – it was said – because the French government felt it to be too 'Germanic' in style. In London, no such accusation could be made and there was a very different feeling. 'When the other street decorations were to be cleared away,' noted the *Spectator* the following year, 'there was a strong popular demand that the Cenotaph should be left.'

Those in authority were less convinced. Sir Alfred Mond, the Liberal MP who was the commissioner of works in Lloyd George's government, wrote a minute to the cabinet in the week after Peace Day expressing his reservations: 'The Monument, although appropriate for the occasion, may not be regarded as sufficiently important and may be of too mournful a character as a permanent expression of the triumphant victory of our arms.' He added: 'There will be probably be a demand for a great and more imposing Monument in any event.'

He had badly misjudged the mood of the nation, assuming triumphalism to be the keynote rather than deep, abiding sorrow. The people's war had ensured that the soldier was now seen as one of the people, no longer just the servant of the establishment, and the people demanded that the national monument recognise the inconceivable price of victory. The idea that the Cenotaph might be 'too mournful' simply made no sense to a nation that was mourning collectively to such a degree.

Lutyens himself understood 'the human sentiment of millions, that the Cenotaph should be as it now is'. It was, he wrote, 'a mass-feeling too deep to express itself more fitly than by the piles of ever-fresh flowers which loving hands placed on the Cenotaph day by day'. Meanwhile Alfred Mond was carping about the flowers being there in the first place: 'A mass of decaying flowers needs almost daily attention, besides tending to attract crowds,' he sniffed. 'I suggest that permission to lay floral tributes be restricted to one or perhaps two days in the year.'

Such attitudes could not prevail, and by the end of July 1919 the cabinet had bowed to public demand and announced that the temporary structure would be remade in stone, though even then there were debates to be had about changes and improvements that might be made. Perhaps, some argued, the four living guardsmen who had stood sentry on the day of the parade could be recreated in bronze, to stand watch for eternity. Maybe the emblems of the major religions practised in the Empire could be carved into the monument, or a suitably all-embracing text from the scriptures added: 'The souls of the righteous are in the Hands of God' was one

Members of the public lay flowers at the Cenotaph in 1920

proposal. Even Lutyens wanted an amendment, suggesting that the Union flag and the banners that had been draped over the structure for the parade be rendered permanent in painted stone. All these ideas were rejected, and it was decided instead simply to produce a copy of the wooden monument in Portland stone, at an estimated cost of around ten thousand pounds. Carved into the stone would be the dates of the conflict, in Roman numerals, and the words: THE GLORIOUS DEAD.

The discussion that ensued about the location of the Cenotaph similarly failed to move public sentiment. 'There is no room for people to gather about it in the midst of the traffic of Whitehall,' insisted *The Times*, and as late as December 1919 Eric Geddes, the minister for transport, was still calling in cabinet for the monument to be located in Parliament Square, rather than in the centre of a major thoroughfare, where it was 'extremely likely to cause accidents'. It was too late. The site had become holy ground for the public and no such relocation could be countenanced. The *Daily Mail*, the country's (and perhaps the world's) biggest selling daily paper, took up the campaign, arguing that the place 'had been consecrated by the tears of many mothers'. Its present location on a busy road was part of its appeal, situating it in the midst of everyday life, not flanked by those pillars of the establishment, the Houses of Parliament and Westminster Abbey. In an era before radio, let alone television, Fleet Street exerted very real influence, and the people's will, expressed largely through the columns of newspapers, carried the day; the Cenotaph would remain in the same place, to be passed by every future prime minister on his or her way from Downing Street to the Commons, a salutary reminder of the price of political failure.

Peace Day was intended to be the final great act of public commemoration, but as the first anniversary of Armistice Day approached, it became apparent that the occasion was not going to pass unmarked. Around the country there were communities planning their own celebrations at all levels of society: a carnival was to be held in East Hoathly, Sussex, and a dance and whist drive in Hatherleigh, Devon, whilst the Albert Hall had been booked for a Victory Ball in aid of charity. No national event, however, was planned, the government going only so far as to announce that the anniversary would not be declared a bank holiday, whilst Lloyd George attempted to politicise the occasion by suggesting that perhaps it might be celebrated as League of Nations Day; it was a proposal that met with the approval of the former prime minister, Herbert Asquith, but attracted little public support.

The official lack of interest in Armistice Day reflected longstanding custom in Britain, which had always been to mark victories in battle, not the moment of peace; Trafalgar Day and Waterloo Day had long been remembered, but not the date of Napoleon's abdication nor even his surrender to British forces. Furthermore, the Armistice had not even been the end of the war, merely a cessation of hostilities, to enable negotiations to begin. For the people, however, it was the day that the suffering stopped, and the resonance of the phrase 'at the eleventh hour of the eleventh day of the eleventh month' meant that it was unlikely to be forgotten.

The need for something to happen on the 11th of November 1919 could not be ignored, though what that something should be remained unclear. The solution came with the mention in high circles of restaging the daily silence held in Cape Town during the war.

In fact, the idea of replicating that practice was not entirely new. The Cape Town silence had barely been noted in the British press, but there were a few who had been profoundly struck by the advent of this strange new custom. Amongst them was Arthur Mercer, a lay churchman who was a resident of Wimbledon and the author of a series of 'Eight Little Booklets for Officers and Others', retailing for a penny each, and including such titles as 'Undoubtedly He Is Coming Again', 'The Supreme Moment of a Lifetime' and 'Will God Really Respond?', the last concerning the need for prayer. In July 1918 Mercer wrote to the *Chelmsford Chronicle*, passing on the news he had received from a South African friend about the ritual being played out daily in Cape Town: 'Passengers in the streets take off their hats, all traffic is stopped for the time being and in the shops the assistants and customers stand still. In Markham's Buildings no sound of the typewriter, telephone, lift bell or a footstep in the corridor is heard. Everyone is referring to the great impression that is made by this silence.' Furthermore, he suggested, this was a practice that could and should be emulated in Britain. 'Could not those who are in positions of authority and influence take the matter up?' he asked.

His plea provoked no response, but, undeterred, he tried again three months later, this time in a letter to the *Essex Herald*: 'If this can be done in Cape Town, is it not possible for it to be repeated in the cities and towns and villages of the United Kingdom? For we have indeed need to mingle our prayers with our praises for the continued success of our arms until victory is won, and then for the great and solemn problems that are going to face us in the future.' This time he did stir up some debate, at least within Essex, where various figures in public life were approached by the press to comment on the idea.

Most expressed themselves cautiously supportive, though the Reverend Canon Lake of Chelmsford held out little hope for such an initiative at a time when the habit of church-going was already being damaged by the protracted nature of the conflict. For, despite the traditional solace offered by the church to the bereaved, the scale of the killing had produced a mounting sense of fatalism, a desire to live in the present with little thought for the future. 'At the request of many, a short midday service of intercession is held on Wednesdays and Fridays,' Lake noted, 'but the attendance has diminished until the recognition of the service has become limited to the faithful few, which is not an encouragement to the lasting influence of any religious observance that interferes in any way with work or pleasure.'

Mercer's proposal soon withered on the vine, but the idea of a national silence was to re-emerge in the spring of 1919. An Australian journalist, Edward Honey, writing under the name Warren Foster, had a letter published in London's *Evening News* on the 8th of May that year. 'Can we not spare some fragment of these hours of peace rejoicing, for a silent tribute to the mighty dead?' he wrote. 'I would ask for five minutes, five little minutes only. Five silent minutes of national remembrance, a very sacred intercession.' He had himself been medically discharged from the Army during the war, and regarded the celebrations of the living as an insult to those who had been killed. Again, though, the suggestion prompted little discussion. When Honey died, a pauper, in 1922, few noticed his passing, save at the Mount Vernon Hospital for Consumption in Northwood, Middlesex, where he had breathed his last; there, in later years, the annual Armistice Day service would include an explanation of the history of the Silence, and note 'the fact that the custom was originated by a patient of the hospital'.

That was overstating the case. Honey's was not the decisive contribution. If there was a single figure to whom the institution of the Silence could be attributed, it was Sir Percy Fitzpatrick, a pro-British South African writer and politician, whose oldest son had been killed in the war. In October 1919, as the first anniversary of the Armistice drew near, he was in London and made approaches both to the prime minister, David Lloyd George, and – through Lord Milner, the former high commissioner for Southern Africa – to the King, suggesting that the daily silence in Cape Town might be replicated throughout the Empire on the 11th of November. 'Silence, complete and arresting, closed upon the city – the moving, awe-inspiring silence of a great cathedral where the smallest sound must seem a sacrilege,' was how Fitzpatrick described Cape Town, as he argued his case. 'Only those who have felt it can understand the overmastering effect in action and reaction of a multitude moved suddenly to one thought and one purpose.'

Lloyd George was said to be enthusiastic about Fitzpatrick's idea and, though George V was initially sceptical, the prime minister was sufficiently persuasive that he won over his monarch. Just five days before the anniversary fell due, the King issued his proclamation, calling on the Silence to be observed. A few months later, as Fitzpatrick prepared to go back home, George V's secretary, Lord Stamfordham, wrote privately to him, acknowledging his contribution: 'The King, who learns that you are shortly returning to South Africa, desires me to assure you that he ever gratefully remembers that the idea of the two minutes' pause on Armistice Day was due to your initiation.'

In public, though, there was no official reference to those who had campaigned for the Silence. The names of Arthur Mercer, Edward Honey and Percy Fitzpatrick, even the name of Lloyd George himself, were not mentioned by the newspapers, and the ritual's roots in Cape Town were overlooked. At a time of social instability, the credit was given instead to the one person who could be seen as a figure of national unity. 'There is left behind,' observed the press, 'the feeling that the King had interpreted the public sentiment more accurately than the public would probably have interpreted it for themselves if left to the guidance of their own judgement.'

So it was that the Silence was inaugurated, centred on the temporary Cenotaph that still stood in Whitehall that November, awaiting its permanent replacement. The rapid establishment of Armistice Day as such a major event was as much a surprise to the government as was the survival of the monument. When Alfred Mond had suggested that the laying of flowers be restricted to two days in the year, the days he had in mind were Easter Monday and the 19th of July, Peace Day. The latter was clearly intended to become the primary anniversary, not Armistice Day, but the unexpected resonance of the first Silence in 1919 changed that perception completely. The people had chosen to mark the day that the guns stopped firing, and they had chosen the monument where they would mark it.

To this great memorial was to be added one more. If the Cenotaph had sought to express the unimaginable numbers of the dead with the symbol of the empty tomb, then the idea of the Reverend Railton of Margate, Kent, was an equally inspired attempt to capture the loss.

David Railton was the son of George Scott Railton (who had been the first Commissioner of the Salvation Army) and, as an Anglican clergyman, he had served as an Army padre in France; he was twice mentioned in dispatches and was awarded the Military Cross for his actions in the trenches at Hill 60 during the first battle of Ypres. In early 1916 he had been billeted in a house near Armentières, the garden of which contained a grave with a rough, white wooden cross on which was written: 'An unknown British Soldier (of the Black Watch)'. How, he wondered, might the family of this anonymous soldier ever be able to mourn their loss? And, as if from nowhere, there came an inspiration: 'Let this body, this symbol of him, be carried reverently over the sea to his native land.' He considered writing to Douglas Haig to suggest such a course of action, before thinking better of it: what difference would such a small gesture make, when the ranks of the nameless dead were growing so remorselessly? The thought, however, remained with him.

Postcard recording the unveiling of the Cenotaph in 1920

After the Armistice, Railton did write to Haig, proposing that a single unidentified body might be brought from the battlefields of France and laid to rest in Westminster Abbey in order to offer a place where those whose loved ones were 'missing, presumed dead', and who therefore had no grave to visit, might pay their respects. He received no reply. Others had made comparable suggestions, including the MPs Horatio Bottomley and Wilfrid Ashley, and had been rebuffed by the government, despite arguing that the French had resolved upon a similar project. 'A thing that appeals most to one nation may not appeal to another,' concluded Andrew Bonar Law, on behalf of the government. 'My belief is that what we have done more truly represents British feeling.'

Railton, however, was not to be discouraged and he tried again, this time approaching Herbert Ryle, the Dean of Westminster, who passed on the suggestion to Lloyd George. The prime minister was keen, partly because it appealed to his sense of populism and partly because, having split the Liberal Party by perpetuating the coalition government, he had little to cling to save that reputation as 'the man who won the war'; keeping alive memories of the conflict was in his political interests. George V, on the other hand, worried that the scheme was 'poised precariously on the tightrope of taste' and that 'one false move and there would be a morbid side-show in the National Shrine'. Apart from anything else, there had already been Peace Day, which had produced the Cenotaph, and the first anniversary of the Armistice, which had brought the Silence. How many more symbols did the country need? But Lloyd George was adamant, and ultimately the King too was persuaded.

In November 1920, therefore, an extraordinary procedure was set in place. Work parties were sent out to the battlefields of Flanders – to the Aisne and the Somme, to Arras and Ypres – where they were charged with exhuming the corpses of four unidentified British soldiers who had died early on in the conflict. (The time of demise was specified to ensure that decomposition would render the remains unrecognisable, and the government allowed for the possibility that the chosen body might be 'cremated, if necessary'.) The cadavers were wrapped in sacks and placed inside a hut in St Pol, where each of the four was covered with a Union flag. At midnight, the senior British officer in France entered the unlit hut with a lantern, touched one of the flags and thereby chose the corpse that was to represent all those whose names and bodies had been separated in death.

As the other three corpses were removed, to be reinterred in a shell hole near the Somme, the selected body was placed in a coffin, made from the wood of an oak in Hampton Court Park, and transported to Boulogne, where Marshal Foch spoke a few words at a final ceremony on French soil. From there it was taken on HMS *Verdun* to Dover, to be greeted by the band of the 2nd Battalion, the Royal Irish Fusiliers playing 'Land of Hope and Glory'. The bandmaster later said that Chopin's 'Marche Funèbre' had been the original choice, but that – with the permission of his commanding officer – he had chosen 'something more martial'.

A special train carriage had been provided to carry the coffin to London where, on the 11th of November 1920, the second anniversary of the Armistice, it formed the centrepiece of a parade through the city, borne on a black gun carriage, drawn by six black horses, and escorted by the most senior officers of the armed forces: five admirals, four field marshals, two generals and an air marshal. The procession stopped at the Cenotaph, where the new, permanent monument was unveiled on the stroke of eleven o'clock by George V. This year the Cenotaph service had taken on a more structured form, and the end of the Silence was marked by the sounding of the Last Post. And then the funeral party, now joined by the King, proceeded on to Westminster Abbey for the re-burial.

The private, secretive nature of the selection of the body was in marked contrast to the French equivalent. There, eight coffins were laid out in the Citadel of Verdun and the public were admitted to pay tribute to the dead. During the final ceremony, attended by disabled veterans and war widows, a private soldier walked around the coffins to the accompaniment of muffled drums and placed a bunch of wild flowers gathered from the battlefield of Verdun on one of the caskets.

The pomp and the ceremony in Britain that accompanied the body's progress was also somewhat removed from Railton's original impulse. His Salvation Army upbringing and his own character did not incline him towards ostentation or displays of wealth and power. He was no pacifist, but his sympathies lay squarely with the soldier rather than the general. 'We want simplicity in our own lives so that we can link them with the simplicity of the workers,' he was later to say. In the aftermath of the 1926 General Strike, he would be found amongst a group of priests trying to bring the miners and mine-owners together, though he encountered opposition, he said, from 'stiff-necked clergy' in the church hierarchy, those whose 'predecessors had tried to stop Wilberforce interfering with slavery'. A somewhat austere figure, who was also wont to complain that 'young people are getting far too many sweets and far too many cinemas', David Railton died in 1955, having never achieved high office in the Church of England. 'But that was the Church's loss,' as a colleague pointed out. 'His heart was too big to be tied to the ecclesiastical machine overmuch.'

The coffin of the Unknown Warrior on the night before the funeral

His legacy was the Tomb of the Unknown Warrior in Westminster Abbey, though he himself would have preferred it to be known as the Tomb of the Unknown Comrade. His contribution was recognised and he was invited to play a part in the service of dedication in 1920. Dressed in chaplain's khaki, he carried the Union flag that was lain over the coffin and then hung above the grave. It was a flag that he had found in No-Man's Land during the war. He had kept it in his haversack, and it had seen service throughout the conflict, 'sometimes being requisitioned as an altar covering, sometimes as a pulpit cloth, and at others to cover the remains of dead soldiers'. On one occasion it was used for the final communion given to a soldier due to be shot at dawn, on another for a service before the battle of the Somme, draped over 'a bucket turned on end in the corner of an old trench'. It was stained with the blood of dead British troops.

The Unknown Warrior was buried in the nave of the Abbey, covered with six barrels of earth from Flanders, and with a slab of Tournai marble placed on top. The Tomb became the shrine that Railton had envisaged, with two hundred thousand visiting it on the first day. And it was venerated at the highest level. In 1921 an Act of Congress was passed to bestow the Congressional Medal of Honor, America's greatest military award, upon the Unknown Warrior. In 1923 Lady Elizabeth Bowes-Lyon married the Duke of York, later to become George VI, in the Abbey, and after the ceremony she laid her bridal bouquet on the Tomb in memory of her older brother, Fergus, who had been killed at the battle of Loos; her action inaugurated a tradition for royal brides that continued into the next century, seen again at the wedding in 2011 of Catherine Middleton and Prince William. It remains the only grave in Westminster Abbey upon which it is forbidden to walk.

And yet, though it was enormously popular at the time, the Tomb of the Unknown Warrior didn't quite live on in the public imagination in the way that the Cenotaph did. It was not intended as a rival to that monument, of course, and in Railton's original conception, it served an entirely different function: not a symbol of all the dead, rather a surrogate son, husband or brother for the bereaved, a focus for the families whose loved ones had no known grave. That was not, though, how Herbert Ryle, the Dean of Westminster who championed Railton's idea, saw it. In a memorandum to the cabinet, Ryle explained that the Tomb 'would do honour to the great mass of fighting men', whilst it would also 'furnish a memorial to them in Westminster Abbey', thereby filling a gap in his own church, for 'At present Westminster Abbey has no memorial of the Great War.' The public embrace of Lutyens's monument had earlier caused the *Church Times* to denounce the cult of 'Cenotapholatry'; now the established church appeared to be seeking its own shrine.

The suspicion that the Tomb was somehow seeking to usurp the Cenotaph as the national memorial was strengthened by the inscription ultimately chosen for the stone. Ryle's first proposal was a simple one:

A BRITISH WARRIOR

WHO FELL IN THE GREAT WAR

1914–1918

FOR KING AND COUNTRY

The dedication on the original stone, at the time of the reburial, was even simpler: AN UNKNOWN WARRIOR. The following year, however, that slab was replaced by another, on which Ryle's original fifteen words had been expanded upon considerably, to produce a central inscription that ran to one hundred and twenty-five, on a far more grandiose scale. It made reference to 'His Majesty King George V', to 'his ministers of state' and to 'the chiefs of his forces', and it carried no suggestion that this was a representative of the unknown dead in particular:

THUS ARE COMMEMORATED THE MANY

MULTITUDES WHO DURING THE GREAT

WAR OF 1914–1918 GAVE THE MOST THAT

MAN CAN GIVE LIFE ITSELF

FOR GOD

FOR KING AND COUNTRY

FOR LOVED ONES HOME AND EMPIRE

FOR THE SACRED CAUSE OF JUSTICE AND

THE FREEDOM OF THE WORLD

The inscription determined the meaning of the Tomb. Its tone of establishment patronage chimed with the original selection process – conducted at dead of night by the most senior officer available – and with the grand ceremony of the re-burial. There was a note of condescension in the idea that this anonymous figure had been elevated that he might 'lie among the most illustrious of the land'. And that hint of arrogance had also been present in Ryle's memorandum to the cabinet. He accepted that some might think the plan 'sensational', before dismissing such concerns: 'But any appeal to national sentiment is open to this charge.' In the whole process, only Railton's flag and the personal reverence of the bereaved had spoken of the ordinary soldier, of the idea that this was a people's war.

Perhaps it was all the associated grandeur that ensured the Tomb failed to retain its power in the same manner as the

Cenotaph. Perhaps it was because it hadn't been there on Peace Day, or for the first Silence. Perhaps it was because it lacked the subtle genius of Lutyens's design. Or perhaps it was because it was removed from the everyday world of the streets, located instead in the grand confines of Westminster Abbey. In France it was different. There the Tomb was placed beneath the Arc de Triomphe, with a much more humble inscription: ICI REPOSE UN SOLDAT FRANÇAIS MORT POUR LA PATRIE 1914–1918. The eternal flame on the grave cast its light upwards, the shadows of humanity flickering over Napoleon's great triumphal arch. In Britain, the meaning seemed to flow in the opposite direction, and the Tomb was overwhelmed by the majesty of its location.

British remembrance was characterised by simplicity and understatement, appealing 'to the English mind, with its fundamental seriousness': the humble origins of the Last Post, played on the most basic of instruments, the spartan plainness of the Cenotaph, the Silence. The latter 'is a far more successful piece of English self-expression than any amount of commemorative oratory', observed the *Manchester Guardian* in 1921. 'It carries into a national rite the individual impulse which made so many last partings wordless at the carriage doors of leave trains.' David Railton's concept of the Unknown Warrior was in that same vein; the execution of his inspiration, however, was not.

Perhaps too it felt different in Britain because the Abbey is a Christian, as well as a national, edifice, and one of the side-inscriptions on the Tomb reflected that other allegiance: 'In Christ shall all be made alive.' At the time, this inscription attracted criticism from some figures in British Jewry, to whom Herbert Ryle replied in an exasperated manner: 'We cannot hope to please everybody.' Pleasing might not have been the right expression; certainly the religious exclusivity, indeed the religious sentiment, detracted from the authority of the monument. The other emblems of remembrance had no such connotations; the previous month a Roll of Honour had been unveiled in Hull to the Jewish war-dead of the city, and the Last Post had been sounded, as it was to be in 1932 when a new Jewish cemetery was opened in Whitefield, Manchester.

The Cenotaph bore no expression of faith, and had been unveiled in an act 'unaccompanied by a religious dedication' because, as Lloyd George said, 'Mohammedans and Hindus were among those in whose memory it stood'. Instead its undoubted spiritual power had been conferred upon it by the people themselves. It 'has become a national shrine not only for the British isles but also for the whole Empire', the prime minister noted, in a letter to Lutyens on the 17th of November 1920, after the unveiling. 'How well it represents the feeling of the nation has been amply manifested by the stream of pilgrims who have passed the Cenotaph during the past week.'

That resort to the image of the pilgrim was not confined to Lloyd George; it was echoed by all observers. In 1920, once the Silence had concluded, and the Unknown Warrior's funeral procession to Westminster Abbey had departed, the barricades in Whitehall were removed to allow the public to pay their own tributes at the Cenotaph. 'We are prepared for the pilgrimage to last three days,' explained the deputy assistant commissioner at Scotland Yard, 'and reliefs for the police have been arranged accordingly. Twenty-five thousand troops and police officers will be employed during the armistice anniversary ceremonies.'

That army of officialdom was deemed necessary to keep moving the vast numbers who came to pay their respects. 'Five days after its unveiling,' marvelled the *Spectator*, 'it was estimated that a million people had visited the Cenotaph. As we write the stream still flows on.' A hundred thousand wreaths were laid on the monument 'in great hedges five feet high', and, it was said, the crowds were so dense in this 'solemn pilgrimage' that 'you could walk across Whitehall over the heads of the people'.

Chapter Five

ALARM

Shrieking upon the Lines the wind blows chill,
Then sadly, as a soul that mourns his friend
Who knows not why he died, nor to what end,
The bugle wails and fades and all is still.

Eric Wearing
'Last Post (The Marine Barracks,
Chatham)' (1931)

At the funeral in November 1914 of Field Marshal Frederick Roberts, the 1st Earl Roberts, who had commanded the British troops in the Boer War, the *Observer* saw the playing of the Last Post as a summons to national unity: 'Those trumpets called all men worthy of a British birthright to put away the things of faction and to rise far above the petty acrimony of our Parliamentary habits in time of peace.' And for the duration of the First World War, the country was indeed mostly united. So too was it in the immediate aftermath, in the delirious excitement of the Armistice. But questions were starting to be asked in some quarters that would ultimately demand answers.

The common language was of 'the fallen', as if soldiers had accidentally stumbled in their passage through life, and of 'the glorious dead', though the voices questioning the exact nature of the 'glory' were becoming louder. Of all the poems entitled 'The Last Post', for example, the best known was that of Robert Graves, written in 1917. If, at the beginning of the century, W.E. Henley had offered a 'tribute to the memory of those who have nobly fallen in their country's cause', Graves gave a very different picture of soldiering in the industrial age:

> O spare the phantom bugle as I lie
> Dead in the gas and smoke and roar of guns,
> Dead in a row with the other broken ones
> Lying so stiff and still under the sky,
> Jolly young Fusiliers too good to die.

First published in his own volume, *Fairies and Fusiliers* (1917), the piece achieved wider currency when reprinted, in a slightly longer form, in the collection *Modern British Poetry* (1920), edited by Louis Untermeyer. Like many of those who had served, Graves was to remain ambivalent about his own experiences in the Army; despite the physical and psychological damage he suffered, and his unflinching portrayal of the war, he remained emotionally attached to the Royal Welch Fusiliers, and at his memorial service in 1985, the Last Post was sounded by a bugler from his old regiment. Yet his work, and that of the other war poets, was to help change attitudes towards the conflict in later years, placing the emphasis on the human cost rather than on the nobility of the cause.

Much of the music composed in the wake of the war was likewise lacking in any form of triumphalism. Ralph Vaughan Williams's *A Pastoral Symphony* (1922), with its evocation in the second movement of a bugler practising and hitting the wrong note, felt elegiac, mourning the dead that the composer had encountered whilst serving in the Royal Army Medical Corps.

Julian Clifford's tone poem *Lights Out* (1919) was similarly a tribute, this time to his friend and fellow composer Ernest Farrar, killed in action the previous year. It began with the bugle call of Lights Out, built to a fortissimo that interwove phrases from the Last Post, and then ended abruptly, 'symbolising the tragic end of a life of great and ever-growing promise'.

Such artistic appropriations of the official forms of commemoration could themselves be absorbed, but nonetheless they represented a break with previous expressions of British culture following a military victory. They suggested that this time things were different, and if they were still a minority pursuit at this stage, their time would come. Of more immediate concern, they emerged in a country where there were signs of grumbling dissatisfaction, of growing discontent with the social order, of a nascent militancy in the workplace. The number of strikes in British industry had fallen dramatically during the war, but it was clear that was just a passing phase. Trade union membership had more than doubled between the outbreak of hostilities and 1920, with the union movement now embracing over eight million workers.

Not included in that number were the country's police officers. Until recently, there had been a National Union of Police and Prison Workers, and in August 1918 eight thousand members of the Metropolitan Police had staged the capital's first and only-ever police strike, which had proved a complete success. The government was sufficiently scared by the thought of a breakdown in law and order, at a time when the Army was otherwise engaged in France, that it conceded every demand. Once that crisis was over, however, a new offer was put together: substantial pay rises combined with the creation, to replace the Union, of the Police Federation, an officially recognised trade association that did not have the right to take industrial action. When, a year on from the London dispute, a national police strike was called, it attracted very little support, save on Merseyside, where the August bank holiday weekend of 1919 became known as the Loot, so widespread was the rioting and the plundering of shops. Troops were sent in, a battleship arrived in the docks, and *The Times* shuddered: 'London Road is the Ypres of Liverpool.'

These events, evoking thoughts of Russia and the Bolshevik revolution of 1917, caused considerable consternation. And there were many more such echoes to be heard if one only listened closely enough. The first full year of peace was also a year of domestic disorder. With a sharp rise in unemployment, a feeling that the construction of 'a land fit for heroes' seemed to be taking a damnably long time coming spilt over into race riots across the country; in Barry, Cardiff, Glasgow, Liverpool, London, Newport and South Shields there were reports of white mobs attacking black and Chinese people, businesses and residences.

More worrying still was the 1919 confrontation in Hyde Park between the police and members of the veterans group, the National Federation of Discharged Sailors and Soldiers, who were holding a demonstration demanding employment. So determined were the protestors to make their point that they broke through a line of mounted police officers and headed for the Houses of Parliament. There they were eventually stopped by a determined police fight-back that was reported excitedly in Moscow: 'The police opened fire. The crowd fled in panic, crushing one another.' That was an exaggeration, as was the claim that six demonstrators had been wounded in the alleged shooting, but the incident – 'only one out of a great many that were taking place all over the country'

— was sufficient to provoke great concern in a country that now contained millions of men trained in the use of firearms. Indeed, many were still in uniform and unhappy with the pace of demobilisation. 'The Army is disaffected and cannot be relied upon,' admitted the prime minister. 'Trouble has occurred already in a number of camps.'

The commemorations of the war sparked their own problems. Peace Day in 1919 was celebrated not only in the parks and streets of London, but in cities and towns across the country. Some had been haughtily dismissive of the idea from the outset: 'A servants' festival,' commented Virginia Woolf, 'something got up to placate and pacify the people.' If that had been the intention, it could not be counted a total triumph. For while the dominant note was one of jubilation, there were also disturbing scenes to be witnessed and dissident voices to be heard. In Glasgow a group of demobilised servicemen staged a demonstration, accompanied by women and children riding on lorries and displaying placards that made clear their position: 'General's widow £25,000; Tommy's widow 13s 9d', read one, and another, somewhat more sarcastically: '400,000 unemployed ex-service men. A grateful country shall never forget you.'

In Manchester the official celebrations were similarly joined by a procession of unemployed ex-servicemen, many wearing their medal ribbons, marching four abreast almost the full length of Oxford Street. Bearing banners that called for justice and employment, they handed out leaflets urging the gathered crowds to 'Honour the dead, remember the living'. At the end of the march, a meeting was held at which speakers spelt out their grievances: 'they had fought for freedom, but the freedom they had won was the freedom to starve'; if the country had found the money to pay them to kill, then 'surely it could find a few thousands for work of a constructive character'. These were not revolutionaries, and they began their meeting by standing, bare-headed, to attention as the Last Post was sounded. But they were unhappy, and they were clear that trouble was on its way. 'Winter was coming, and winter, with its cold and hunger, meant riots,' a speaker was reported as saying, and it was intended as a warning, rather than a threat.

Elsewhere in the country, the riots were already starting. In Leicester a strike by hosiery workers flared into 'deplorable scenes of violence', as they were described in the press. 'Factory windows have been broken by hostile crowds, employers have been stoned in taxicabs and a private house a mile out of the town attacked, and the windows smashed late at night.' This was a long way removed from the stillness and reverence at the Cenotaph. And Leicester was no isolated case.

The worst of the violence on Peace Day came in Luton, where feelings had been running high all week, after the local council refused permission for discharged soldiers to hold a memorial service in the public park. Further provocation was caused by the announcement that a 'peace banquet' was to be held for the great and good of the community. When the mayor attempted to read out a proclamation from the steps of the town hall at the start of the official celebrations, he was interrupted by booing and hissing, and finally stopped altogether by a group of ex-servicemen who mounted the steps and angrily denounced the inadequacy of their pensions.

This sparked an invasion of the town hall by a large crowd who 'proceeded to break the chairs and tables and to throw them through the windows'. The bunting and decorations were torn down, and the wires to the illuminations were cut, before a fire was started that threatened to raze the building to the ground. The fire brigade was summoned, but 'the mob took possession of the motor engines when they arrived, preventing the firemen from getting to work. Others raided a neighbouring motor garage for petrol, which they poured onto the building. When at last the firemen got into position they found that large sections of their hose had been cut.' In the ensuing street battles, a police baton charge was met by a hail of bottles, leading to the hospitalisation of several officers. Fourteen firemen and over a hundred of the crowd were also injured, the town hall was destroyed and the damages ran to an estimated quarter of a million pounds. Councillors were left protesting that it had all been a misunderstanding: 'There was no lack of sympathy on the part of the council with the discharged soldiers.'

There were further, less serious confrontations in Luton the following night, but by then the focus of events had shifted elsewhere. A major outbreak of rioting in Coventry took place on Sunday, the day after Peace Day – 'a mob of men broke the windows of dozens of shops, looted a boot-shop and took clothes from another tradesman's premises' – followed by more troubles on the next day.

That Monday the violence spread, fuelled by specific local circumstances. In Swindon there had been complaints about the erection of a flagstaff outside the town hall 'at considerable expense to the ratepayers'. The pole was set on fire and burnt to the ground, and 'a crowd attacked the police station, smashing three large windows, and also attacked several business places'. In Bilston, meanwhile, the populace decided to take its revenge on one particularly hated police officer. A crowd, some thousands strong, surrounded the police station and, having demolished a wall to provide ammunition, began throwing bricks at the windows. Improvised battering rams were used to try to smash down the locked doors and, when that didn't work, petrol was poured on the building and set on fire. That attempt also failed.

There was disorder too in Ireland. In Cork, clashes between British soldiers and Sinn Féin activists – the latter tearing down patriotic emblems for the Peace Day celebrations – had an explicitly political intent. So too did the disturbances in Dublin where republican students from the National University clashed with loyalists from Trinity College. But in Londonderry there was no such political motivation on display; instead, a mob raided Watt's Distillery and began dishing out free whiskey to all-comers. When the police intervened, they were 'vigorously stoned all the way to the police station'.

For the most part, these incidents were reported as being entirely unconnected, though underlying them there did seem to be a common grievance against heavy-handed officialdom, combined with a feeling that the people's voice was not being heard. And perhaps too the celebrations themselves fuelled the sense of anger. 'The tendency of the people to rejoice is an affront and an offence to all who, for the moment, from many divergent causes, are labouring under a sense of grievance and injustice,' observed the *Derby Daily Telegraph*, one of the few papers that attempted to make sense of the riots. 'It is bitterly resented, and by way of demonstrating the fact that they feel no inclination to take part in what they deem the hollow mockery of Peace Rejoicings, they have resorted to excesses which are foolish and without an atom of justification.'

Britain was not alone amongst the allied nations in witnessing such clashes. In the years immediately following the peace, there were also riots, disturbances and even attempted uprisings in Germany, Belgium, Italy and France. The morning after the first Armistice Day commemorations, later in 1919, there were reports in the British press from America, where a long-running dispute in Centralia, Washington, had erupted into violence between the Industrial Workers of the World (the radical trade union commonly known as the Wobblies) and the local chapter of the newly founded veterans organisation, the American Legion. 'Strikers belonging to the Industrial Workers of the World fired upon an armistice parade yesterday, killing three and wounding many,' read the British accounts. In fact, the final tally was six dead – four members of the Legion, one of the IWW and a deputy sheriff – and the sequence of events, particularly the question of who started the violence that day, remains the subject of some dispute. What is certain is that the Centralia Massacre contributed heavily to the Red Scare in America, centring on the political inclinations of the IWW and other unions.

The fear of communism was likewise evident in Britain. Even as the news was coming in from Centralia, Winston Churchill, then secretary of state for air, was being asked in Parliament about casualty figures for servicemen involved in the Russian Civil War, where Britain supported those fighting to remove the Bolshevik government; his reply revealed that there were thus far 181 British dead and a further 190 missing or taken prisoner. By the standards of the Western Front, these were perhaps negligible numbers, but nonetheless they were still war-dead and their deaths didn't quite fit with the image of a nation now at peace. There were many who felt that, in the wake of 'the war to end all wars', there was something wrong about sending British troops to resist a workers' revolution.

For most people, however, the argument over international politics was of less immediate concern than was the welfare of the demobilised forces. This showed no signs of abating as the months and years wore on and as conditions failed to improve. Former soldiers were again to be seen begging on the streets, just as they had been a century earlier in the wake of Waterloo. In Portsmouth in 1921 'a large body of unemployed demonstrated outside the workhouse,' it was reported, 'declaring that they were starving.' In Manchester a report by ex-servicemen's associations in the winter of that year drew attention to the conditions that unemployed veterans and their families were enduring, 'not only destitute but absolutely on the verge of starvation'; charities in the city had received eight thousand applications for assistance, but had managed to help just seven hundred. And in the London Borough of Islington, where seven thousand people were registered as unemployed, a demonstration was staged at the town hall in January 1921, broken up by mounted police. Officials later claimed that 'a number of men carried pieces of iron rail concealed about their clothing and that some had firearms'. The mayor took an even firmer line, insisting that 'the demonstrators were not genuine unemployed, but were unemployables'.

Elsewhere, when a memorial tablet was unveiled to the forty-six members of the Lancaster Battery of the West Lancashire Royal Field Artillery who had died in the war, Lieutenant-Colonel Wilson, the commanding officer of the battery, spoke out on behalf of those who survived the conflict: 'They came back, after receiving only 1s 2d per day, to find those people whom they had left at home rolling in money.'

The main issue was unemployment, a fact identified by David Railton. In 1921, using the authority he had gained from initiating the Tomb of the Unknown Warrior, he tried to bring the newspapers' attention to the plight of unemployed veterans by demonstrating it in action. 'I dressed myself in

Ex-servicemen demand employment, 1919

ragged clothes and motored into Carlisle,' he explained afterwards. 'From there I tramped round the farmhouses, asking for work of any kind.' His conclusions saddened him. 'My conviction is that it is almost impossible to get even an hour's work,' he reflected. 'It certainly seems that the chances of ex-service men seeking work are almost hopeless.'

For those afflicted by this sense of hopelessness, it was often Armistice Day that became the focus of the complaints. Even Railton's best-known initiative attracted adverse comment; a group of unemployed workers in Taunton denounced the pomp surrounding the burial of the Unknown Warrior 'whilst living heroes were being denied the right to live'. It was a sentiment echoed in the pages of the *Daily Herald* on the day of the interment: 'While the great pageant is thus used for the emotional doping of the people, other and named victims, hundreds and thousands of them, plead in vain for even what they had before the war. They are workless, they beg in the streets.' The same Taunton group also passed a resolution objecting to the erection of a war memorial in the town, suggesting instead that the best tribute to the dead would be a house-building programme to provide both decent accommodation for veterans and jobs for the living. They pressed their point by staging a parade on Armistice Day in 1920 to collect money for distressed families.

Such demonstrations were to become a familiar sight at Armistice Day celebrations over the next couple of years. In Reading in 1921 a procession bore a banner reading 'The dead are remembered, but we are forgotten'. In Liverpool that year, two hundred ex-soldiers, carrying a banner that read 'Bread, not Medals', interrupted the Silence with 'a violent babel of cat-calls' and shouts of 'What we want is food, not prayers' and 'Anybody want a medal?' Some of those in the crowd tried to silence them. 'The position became very ugly, and the police looked on with anxiety,' it was reported, 'but happily decency triumphed, and after half a minute's discordance the last of the disturbing voices died away.'

Meanwhile, in Dundee, unemployed workers sang 'The Red Flag' during the Silence and gave three cheers for James Connolly, hero of the Irish republican movement and member of the International Workers of the World, who had been executed in 1916. The noise was loud enough to drown out the sounding of the Last Post, and on this occasion the crowd took more direct action. In the ensuing brawl, 'The red flag was torn and trampled upon, and many a hard blow was exchanged, ex-service men taking a prominent part in the proceedings.' The leader of the demonstration was subsequently given sixty days in jail for disturbing the peace.

Most powerful of all in 1921 was an unofficial parade on the afternoon of Armistice Day at the Cenotaph. Several thousand unemployed veterans marched down Whitehall, carrying wreaths which were laid on the monument whilst ex-soldiers stood to attention and saluted the dead. The police took it upon themselves to remove those wreaths that were deemed to be inappropriate, objecting to some of the more explicitly political inscriptions. 'To those who died and were not forgotten, from those who live and are forgotten', read one; 'In memory of victims of capitalism who died, from victims of capitalism who are starving', spelt out another; 'To the victims of capitalism, who gave their lives for rent, interest and profit, from the survivors of the peace, who are suffering worse than death for the same unholy trinity', ran a third. Many of those on the march wore the medals they had been awarded on active service, but it was noted that some wore instead on their left breast a row of pawn tickets. It is hard to imagine a more dignified or graphic symbol of the straits to which veterans of the war had been reduced.

When confined to a peaceful protest in this manner, the political and humanitarian message could attract support. There were, after all, many millions who knew and understood the grievances that were being aired. But disturbances such as those in Dundee, when the crowds felt that their sacred rites were being desecrated, were also not uncommon.

The most widely reported incident came in 1920 when the Silence was interrupted in Fleet Street, London, by noises emanating from the offices of the communist newspaper the *Workers Dreadnought*, a publication founded and edited by Sylvia

Pankhurst (though she herself was in jail at the time). 'Girls seemed to be dancing and singing on a table in front of the window, in full view of the street,' said one member of the public. 'They were making a most awful noise.' The women working in the office gave a slightly different account: 'We were dusting the office. We certainly made some noise, but we did not dream of people outside hearing.' They did, however, happily accept that the Silence meant nothing to them: 'We were not interested, as we don't believe in it.' No action was taken until the end of the Silence, at which point a large crowd forced their way into the offices. Finding that the offenders were all female, the men were overtaken by a spirit of chivalry and stood back to let the women in the crowd take over. 'Some girls knocked us about,' explained one of the women from the *Workers Dreadnought*. 'They kept on hitting us until the police came.'

The paper's staff, though, were not alone in expressing their dissent, even as early as 1920. As the vast crowds gathered that year to visit the new Cenotaph and the Tomb of the Unknown Warrior, they were mocked by small groups gathering on the plinth of Nelson's Column, which, it was reported, was 'being used as a platform for revolutionary and seditious speeches against the Crown and commonwealth and often outraging national sentiment'.

It was not the politics that caused offence to the general public, so much as the disrespect shown to the Silence and the implied slur on those who had died. In 1924 a twenty-eight-year-old seaman from Great Yarmouth was taken into custody for his own safety after walking down the Strand during the Silence with his hat on, an action that led to him being assaulted by the crowd. He was charged with insulting behaviour likely to cause a breach of the peace, and was bound over. His defence was that he had done nothing illegal and that, in a free country, he should have the liberty to walk down the street if he so chose. 'Why all these demands?' he asked. 'It is not an order. People can please themselves.' Similarly in Shepherd's Bush, West London, in 1928: 'a young man who had refused to take off his hat was struck on the nose by a man in the crowd, and with great difficulty the police formed a cordon round the young man until he was able to board a bus.' There was no political dimension to these acts of dissent, but they provoked the same response from ordinary people as had the *Workers Dreadnought* women eight years earlier.

Viewed from the position of the state, however, the politics mattered very much indeed. The fear that the taint of Bolshevism might infect the working class was taken seriously. There were groups in the country, argued Winston Churchill in 1919, who wished 'to provoke an outbreak in the form of a mutiny or general strike, or preferably both together, in the hope that a general smash and overthrow of society may result'. Such people sought to forge links between soldiers, ex-servicemen and workers, 'to weld them altogether, to rouse them altogether, to make a general overthrow on the Russian model'. His sentiments were echoed in Conservative newspapers around the country over the next couple of years, as they issued dire warnings that 'the agents and sympathisers of Lenin and Trotsky in this country are seeking to organise the unemployed into a striking force for the red revolution', the consequence of which would be 'the forcible establishment of Bolshevist minority tyranny'.

These fears grew with the rising tide of industrial militancy. In 1921, with the ranks of the unemployed now exceeding two million — the majority of whom were ex-servicemen — the government's response to a national coal strike was the declaration of the first state of emergency, under the Emergency Powers Act passed the previous year. Over eighty-five million working days were lost to industrial action in 1921, more than twice the number recorded in any previous year of the century. Meanwhile, more violent matters were being resolved in Ireland. Sinn Féin's declaration of independence in 1919 had prompted a heavy-handed response by the British government, escalating into a bitter war that left over two thousand dead. But with the signing of the Anglo-Irish Treaty in December 1921, British rule in what would become the Irish Free State came to an end, offering a hopeful precedent for would-be revolutionaries in what remained of the United Kingdom.

The rival meanings of remembrance were to play a central role in defusing such dissent. The government's immediate response at the end of the war had been to celebrate victory, but that had clearly failed to mesh with the emotions of the people, and, in response, concessions had been made on the permanence of the Cenotaph and on the marking of Armistice Day. Yet the public mood was not by any means uniform. There was grief, but there was also anger; on the one hand, there were the families of 'Our Glorious Dead', and then there were the survivors, the ex-servicemen whom the *Daily Express* was later (when society had settled down a little) to refer to as 'Our Glorious Living'. The latter were more immediately threatening to national stability, and, if triumphalism had proved not to be appropriate, then mourning was at least a more palatable option than was open revolt.

Consequently, during the 1920s, the focus of official ceremonies was adjusted gradually but definitively, to mute the expression of the veterans' demands for social justice in favour of the silent sorrow of the bereaved, thus placing personal

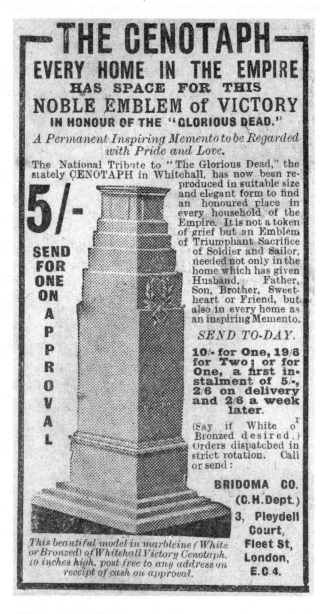

The mawkish side of remembrance: an advertisement for a ten-inch-high replica of the Cenotaph, made of marbleine

emotion rather than political dissatisfaction at the centre of remembrance. The groundswell of feeling that had been articulated through the Silence — against the instincts of the establishment — was now to be formalised, given shape by those in authority who recognised the danger and were prepared to adapt in the face of the discontent. Anger could be contained if its potential allies were subsumed into a national mood of mourning.

Much emphasis was placed upon the idea that the country, and the Empire beyond, was in essence a family, at the head of which was the King, the hero of the silver badge parade, the creator — it was supposed — of the Silence, and the man who had represented the peoples of the Empire as the 'chief mourner' of the Unknown Warrior (indeed he was the only person to be named on the Tomb). 'Today's act of remembrance is shared by the entire imperial family of Britain,' noted the *Dundee Courier* of the Cenotaph service in 1926, and similar expressions became commonplace. This extended metaphor of the national household undoubtedly provided comfort for many of the bereaved. Kate Shallis, of Harlesden, London, who had lost four sons in the war, attended the Cenotaph ceremony in 1927 and found some peace: 'I felt that the King and Queen and I and the masses of people were just one big family, thinking together the same dear thoughts of our million sons who died for us.'

Whilst those who had suffered such losses were being feted and honoured by the state, there remained the mass of ex-servicemen, amongst whom there was no uniform mood. Some were becoming politicised, finding channels through which to voice their resentment over pensions and unemployment, but there were other, less divisive, impulses that might be harnessed: the deep bonds of comradeship forged in the trenches, and the discipline that came from the men's military training. The characteristics of 'blind obedience and an entire submission to the orders of their commanding officer', identified by William Pulteney nearly two centuries earlier, still survived; in the British Army the bugle call remained 'the voice of the King'. If these attributes could be brought to the fore, then the inclination towards rebelliousness would surely fade.

Amongst those most alarmed by the riots and the demonstrations was Field Marshal Douglas Haig, who saw the problem as stemming, in part, from the plethora of ex-servicemen's associations. Some of these he considered to be dangerously left-wing in their thinking, and he set about trying to bring them all together under a more responsible leadership.

There were, by the end of the war, several veterans' organisations, including the radical, campaigning groups the National Association of Discharged Sailors and Soldiers, and the similarly titled National Federation of Discharged and Demobilised Sailors and Soldiers. The latter — whose battle with the police was to be so enthusiastically reported in the Moscow press — fielded a candidate in the 1917 by-election in Abercromby, Liverpool, attracting a quarter of the votes cast. The same year the Comrades of the Great War, a more conservative grouping, was founded by the secretary of state for war, the Earl of Derby, with Haig as its first life member. Between them, these three bodies, all representing non-commissioned soldiers, sponsored some thirty or so candidates — known collectively as the Silver Badge Party — in the 1918 general election; just one candidate was elected, taking his seat as an independent Conservative.

There was also, most radical of all, the National Union of Ex-Service Men. Founded in 1919, the Union called for better pensions, particularly for disabled veterans, and for all ex-servicemen to be reimbursed the differential between what they had actually been paid and what they would have been paid had they enjoyed the higher rates of remuneration available in the Australian Army. It suggested funding these demands by nationalising land ownership, whilst also denouncing the government's actions in Ireland and calling for a rent strike. The Union thus had a political dimension that extended beyond the veterans themselves, and it allied itself to the Labour Party and to the industrial trade unions. 'Ex-service men organising according to no-party lines and keeping apart from the Labour movement were playing into the hands of the tin-hats and capitalists of the country,' argued Alexander Scott, a leading member. Another, G.F. Simmons, was sure that if the millions of ex-servicemen 'got together with organised labour there was no government in power or ever likely to be who could stop their demands'. At its height, the Union claimed – a little implausibly – two hundred thousand members, but its national structure dissolved itself in 1920, leaving a handful of groups who were assimilated into parties of the Left.

Beyond the other ranks, there were further organisations representing former officers, which were brought together by Haig in 1919 to form the Officers' Association. Thus began the process of consolidation that culminated in 1921 with the creation of the British Legion, subsuming all the existing bodies into a single entity with Haig elected as its president.

The Legion, as it was familiarly known, was larger than its predecessors, but still represented only a minority of ex-servicemen; its inter-war peak of four hundred thousand members, reached in 1938, was less than a tenth of the number who had served in uniform in the First World War. It was a conservative, establishment organisation from the outset, and it was immediately recognised by the government – with a sense of relief – as the only legitimate representative of ex-servicemen. 'The ex-Service Associations should be represented by a contingent not exceeding 200 men,' it was decided, as preparations were being made for the 1921 Cenotaph service, 'and these should be chosen as follows: 150 men by the British Legion, representative of all Branches of the Services which are incorporated in that body, and 50 by the Admiralty, representative of the various naval and mercantile ex-Service Associations not included in the British Legion.'

The new body inherited the role of campaigning for a better deal for veterans, even if it pursued its demands through formal representation rather than demonstrations on the streets, but it added a strong community element, setting up social clubs around the country. Through this network, the comradeship of ex-servicemen, it was hoped, would express itself in civic virtues: 'loyalty, unity, right, justice, peace and mutual cooperation', as the Conservative minister Lord Salisbury put it when opening the Barnet branch of the Legion in 1923. 'They were the principles which had made England great in the past, and upon them alone her future greatness depended.' Thus were members of the Legion encouraged also to feel part of the great imperial family, to be proud of their military service and of the values inculcated in the ranks.

The acceptance by the establishment was entirely as Haig had intended and, towards the end of his life, he made a speech explaining that, in his view, 'the Legion had saved this country from bloodshed during the critical years since the Armistice'. Some of the groups that were absorbed into the Legion, he was reported to have said, 'were Bolshevist in intention, and they were better with him than with their Bolshevist leaders. They had had machine-guns, arms and munitions.' He added: 'I got these organisations into the British Legion, and the Bolshevist organisations were broken up.' He was almost certainly exaggerating the radical inclinations of the ex-servicemen's bodies, but his argument spoke eloquently of the fear that stalked the land in those first years of peace. There was also a note of defensive belligerence as he staked his claim; he made the speech in the aftermath of the 1926 General Strike, during which he had faced criticism from some in the Legion when he called on members to step in and help the authorities maintain public services.

There had been no true revolutionary moment in that time, however. 'Unless,' wrote the Glasgow-based Labour leader Manny Shinwell, 'a demand to deal with unemployment, rid ourselves of the slums and raise the standard of living could be regarded as revolutionary.' Nonetheless, the anger felt by so many had threatened the stability of the country, and the creation of the Legion did much to isolate the more disruptive elements and to silence those voices that the establishment had no desire to answer.

Chapter Six

FALL IN

Solemn the drums thrill; Death august and royal
Sings sorrow up into immortal spheres.
There is music in the midst of desolation
And a glory that shines upon our tears.

Laurence Binyon
'For the Fallen' (1914)

One of Douglas Haig's primary concerns as president of the British Legion was to refocus energy away from political campaigning, and instead to work to improve the provision of charity for ex-servicemen. One initiative in particular, the Legion's Appeal Fund, commonly known as the Haig Fund, was to become personally associated with him, though in fact it predated the Legion itself. Launched in 1920 by the Officers' Association, the Fund had sparked a myriad of local events, including benefit concerts, golf tournaments, fancy dress balls and special cinema screenings, even if the Jockey Club did decide against the suggestion of staging an extra day's flat racing for the charity. On the formation of the British Legion, the Fund was taken over by the new body, but there was a general feeling that it could go still further if, as Haig and others argued, the project could acquire a focus, a symbol that would make some unified sense of all the activity.

The result was announced in a press release from the Legion in October 1921, which called for 'the wearing of a Flanders poppy as a sign of remembrance and reverence to the many thousands of our heroes who rest beneath this flower in Flanders fields'. These poppies, made of blood-red silk (or cotton, depending on price) were to be sold on Armistice Day itself by women in the streets, and any profits that accrued would 'be used to alleviate the distress among ex-servicemen', though only those who had served during the most recent war. The announcement went on to note: 'There is an added value to these poppies in the fact that they are made by the women and children in the devastated areas of France.' And, it was urged, 'On every memorial – city, town or village – a wreath of poppies should be placed.'

The red corn poppy had become a familiar sight on the battlefields of northern Europe, growing in great profusion on land that had been churned up and fertilised with the blood and bones of millions of men. Even during the course of the hostilities, combatants had noted something symbolic in the simple, enduring beauty of nature in the midst of the slaughter. 'Clumps of crimson poppies,' wrote the British fighter pilot, Cecil Lewis, describing what he saw from his aeroplane, 'thrusting out from the lips of craters, straggling in drifts between the hummocks, undaunted by the desolation, heedless of human fury and stupidity.'

That symbolism spread from the Western Front back home with the publication in December 1915 of a poem by Lieutenant-Colonel John McCrae of the Canadian Army Medical Corps. McCrae was a veteran of the Boer War and, despite having long since left the forces, he immediately re-enlisted when war was declared in 1914, serving until his death from pneumonia in January 1918. His poem, 'In Flanders

Fields', prompted the renaming of the flower to become the Flanders poppy, and ended with a challenge to others to continue the fight in which he and his comrades were presently engaged:

> Take up our quarrel with the foe:
> To you from failing hands we throw
> The torch; be yours to hold it high.
> If ye break faith with us who die
> We shall not sleep, though poppies grow
> In Flanders fields.

The poem was successful throughout the English-speaking world, including in America, a nation that was then yet to join the war. And it was in America that Moina Belle Michael, a schoolteacher from Georgia, read McCrae's words and, after hostilities had ceased, responded to his challenge by launching a campaign to have the poppy adopted as the symbol of those who had been killed in the conflict. The initial design that was used, however, was unsuccessful. A torch of liberty entwined with a poppy and adorned with colours from the flags of the Allies, it was given the name the Flanders Victory Memorial Flag, and it failed to inspire: too confused, too fussy and perhaps too triumphalist in its celebration of victory. Reverting simply to the poppy itself, Michael persuaded first the Georgia branch of the American Legion to adopt it as their memorial emblem and then, through them, the whole of that organisation; the proposal was ratified in 1920.

Also championing the cause was Anna Guérin, a Frenchwoman who had begun manufacturing silken poppies shortly after the Armistice. She similarly campaigned for the flower to be adopted as a symbol by all the Allied countries, and in 1921 she visited London, where she convinced the British Legion, and Haig in particular, to take up the poppy.

The arrival of the emblem in Britain struck an immediate chord with the public: the initial order was for two million poppies to be made, and when it became clear that that was an underestimate, a further six million were ordered, and still 'these were not half enough'. In that first year, over a hundred thousand pounds was raised for the Fund, an amount doubled the following year and tripled by 1924. Even so, it could hardly hope to address the scale of the need. Haig himself explained in 1925 that there were half a million disabled men in the country, with an unemployment rate of ten per cent, three hundred thousand children who had lost a parent, and a hundred and sixty thousand widows, the latter in receipt of 'often inadequate' pensions.

Nonetheless, the success of the first year was such that in 1922, production was brought home from the war-widows of France. A factory was set up in the East End of London which employed only disabled veterans and which, within a couple of years, was making nearly thirty million of the emblems annually. Demand was so high that in 1926 production was moved to newly built premises in Richmond, complete with a block of flats to house the workers; by 1939, some four hundred disabled men were working to produce the poppies sold by three hundred and sixty thousand volunteers. Various models were by now available, from the simple to the ornate, with minimum prices set between one penny and half-a-crown across the range. It had become by far the best-known charity flag-day in the calendar; Armistice Day itself was increasingly referred to as Poppy Day, and there was an 'almost universal wearing of the Flanders poppy'.

Douglas Haig visits the British Legion's poppy factory in Richmond

Haig's introduction to Britain of the Poppy – joining the Silence, the Cenotaph, the Unknown Warrior and the Last Post – was the last major addition to the national symbolism that had grown up around remembrance. But it was still some time before the various elements were formalised. In 1919 the crowds outside St Paul's Cathedral had sung 'O God, Our Help in Ages Past', the hymn that was to become most closely associated with remembrance, at the conclusion of the Silence, but there was no uniformity, and elsewhere other hymns were chosen, including 'Old Hundredth', 'Rock of Ages' and 'Peace, Perfect Peace'. Some standardisation was to be expected.

Similarly, although the Last Post was sounded at the Cenotaph in 1920 to mark the end of the Silence, it was not yet a fixture of the order of service. In this instance, however, if the establishment had its way, the call would not become such a fixture, for its note of loss, its funereal tone, was considered out of place in what should be considered a celebration.

In 1921 a cabinet committee was convened under the chairmanship of Lord Curzon, now the foreign secretary, to determine how the Cenotaph service should be structured, in the hope that what they decided 'will become a type for the future'. Starting from the principle that 'it is undesirable that the ceremony should be too elaborate', the conclusion was that maroons should be fired on the last stroke of Big Ben as it rang the hour at eleven o'clock, with further maroons two minutes later. There would then be the singing of 'O God, Our Help in Ages Past' and the sounding of Reveille. There was no mention of the Last Post, an absence explained by the committee's insistence that 'as Armistice Day is not a day of national grief, but rather a commemoration of a great occasion in the national history, it is undesirable to lay stress upon the idea of mourning.'

That was not how the people saw it. A day of national grief was precisely what Armistice Day represented, and it was not complete without the Last Post. But there were those who genuinely felt that the sounding of the call was not appropriate at memorial services. 'That, surely, ought only to be done at the actual time of burial,' argued the Reverend W.F. Armstrong of Leverton, Lincolnshire, though he was content with the other call used on such occasions: 'The sounding of the Reveille stands upon quite a different footing, for it is a reminder of Our Lord's words to Martha: "Thy brother shall rise again."' In 1923 it was indeed Reveille that was again used to end the Silence at the Cenotaph, with the Last Post absent.

The fact, though, that there was a service at all at the Cenotaph that year was the key issue. For in 1923, Armistice

Day fell on a Sunday for the first time since the war, and that changed the nature of the event entirely, at least as far as the establishment was concerned. In previous years, the Sunday immediately prior to Armistice Day had been marked with an official state service of remembrance in Westminster Abbey, starting at half past ten and attended by the King and Queen. In 1923 this would necessarily clash with the Cenotaph ceremony, and the government decided to take soundings about how to proceed. The nature of the consultation process hinted at the probable outcome, the cabinet resolving that the foreign secretary 'should consult the Archbishop of Canterbury and should afterwards approach the King'.

Unsurprisingly, the conclusion was that there would be no gathering at the Cenotaph that year, though the cabinet noted that 'This should not prejudice the arrangements in future years when Armistice Day did not fall on a Sunday.' It also, a little grudgingly, conceded that 'the laying of wreaths by the general public at the Cenotaph should be allowed throughout the day, under the usual supervision of the police in the interests of order'.

Instead of the Cenotaph ceremony, it was announced, there would be a public service in Trafalgar Square at three o'clock on the Sunday afternoon, conducted by the Reverend H.R.L. Sheppard (Dick Sheppard, as he was universally known), the 'eloquent and energetic vicar' of St Martin-in-the-Fields. The gathering would be addressed by Stanley Baldwin and Stanley Bruce, prime ministers of the UK and Australia respectively, and would feature the massed bands of the Coldstream and Welsh Guards.

No sooner had these arrangements been disclosed than there was a storm of protest, expressed not merely in London but in newspapers around the country. 'This by no means satisfies the sentiments of a large section of the public,' insisted the *Derby Daily Telegraph*, whilst the *Dundee Courier* argued that the Cenotaph service was 'an annual custom which has become sanctified into a kind of public sacrament'. The *Western Daily Press* was more forthright: it was an 'amazingly fatuous suggestion' to discard so lightly 'a sacrament with the man and the woman in the street'.

The service at Westminster Abbey was seen as being exclusive, it did not allow public participation, it was merely the established church and the state talking to each other without reference to, or apparent interest in, the people. 'Admission will be by ticket only,' it was announced, 'but the tickets will be distributed from the chief departments of the State.' The Cenotaph, on the other hand, was the nation's own shrine, with a unique charge that touched all who contemplated it: 'It makes you shiver,' as one woman put it. And the sop of the Trafalgar Square gathering was clearly inadequate – there was no connection between that place and the war-dead – and anyway it was not to be held at the eleventh hour: there was no significance to the hour of three o'clock. The entire edifice of remembrance that had been built up over the last five years was in danger of being knocked down by an establishment that had simply failed to recognise the importance of the people's own symbols.

More than that, the government's decision put in jeopardy the delicate, unspoken balance that existed between the two rival claims to the custodianship of remembrance, symbolised by the figures that were always present at a soldier's funeral: the padre and the bugler. The former represented the traditional source of solace and comfort for the bereaved, with his language of sacrifice and salvation. The latter was seen to speak only of loss and death for, though the Last Post might be followed by the spiritual rebirth of Reveille, it was clear that the second call meant very little in terms of public culture; the bugler was associated solely with the sounding of the Last Post.

And it was the bugler with his secular spirituality and – despite his military status – with the democracy of his call, who seemed better able to articulate the nation's response to the war. 'Those who went to church,' the *Daily Express* had observed, in the wake of the first Silence, 'missed the stupendous thrill and mystery of the greater service in which men and women confronted their God, held communion without the hindrance of formula.' For four years the churches had held remembrance services which were well attended but which did not begin to rival the power of a Silence that could halt all human activity in the midst of a working day. Now the two had come into direct competition, and the government's first instinct was to back the padre against the bugler, not noticing that the country had changed.

Amongst those protesting at the abandonment of the Cenotaph in 1923 was General Bramwell Booth, the head of the Salvation Army, who wrote to Lord Curzon saying that, if the established church didn't wish to hold a ceremony, he himself was 'prepared to make all arrangements for a Cenotaph service on the lines of those which the Salvation Army has previously conducted at the Mansion House and elsewhere'.

Confronted by cries of outrage – described in cabinet minutes as 'strong public opinion' – the state began the process of backing down. A representative of Westminster Abbey explained to the press that he personally supported the idea of a Cenotaph service being held as well, though 'it might be difficult to get an adequately trained choir to lead the singing of the hymns' because, of course, 'it is obviously impossible for the choir and clergy to be at the Cenotaph when there must be service in the Abbey.' He also, somewhat defensively and a little unconvincingly, denied an allegation that there were those in the church hierarchy who regarded the Cenotaph as 'a pagan memorial'. (The same sentiment had been expressed in November 1921 by Lieutenant-General George Macdonogh when he denounced the poppy as 'a pagan flower'.)

Within days, the government had overturned its own decision. The cabinet was 'deeply impressed,' it was said, 'by the volume of public feeling against the suspension this year of the Cenotaph ceremony, and there was general agreement that the desire of the public should be met'. Further, 'many members of the cabinet were inclined to think, on reflection, that the original decision was a mistaken one.' The greatest fear was almost certainly the one hinted at in a remark that 'if no official service was held, the public at the Cenotaph would be certain to organise an impromptu one.' The only way to contain the people's emotion was to take the service back into state ownership.

And so a compromise was reached. The King and Queen, together with the prime minister and dignitaries from the Empire and the armed forces, attended the service in the Abbey, where the Silence was observed, the Archbishop of Canterbury preached a sermon and the monarch laid a wreath on the Tomb of the Unknown Warrior. Meanwhile the Prince of Wales and his younger brother, the Duke of York, went to the Cenotaph for a service presided over by the Bishop of London. This included — for the first time at the monument — a Christian prayer, this being justified 'as Armistice Day fell on a Sunday'; the beachhead thus established by the church was not subsequently to be relinquished.

In 1928, the next time that Armistice Day fell on a Sunday, the home secretary, William Joynson-Hicks, wrote a memorandum to the cabinet, reminding members what had happened five years previously: 'So soon as the proposed arrangements were announced in the press there was so much public outcry at the abandonment of the service at the Cenotaph that the decision had to be reconsidered and eventually two services were held.' He concluded: 'My own feeling is that the procedure adopted in 1923 was somewhat of a mistake and it would be better this year to observe Armistice Day in the customary manner, the main ceremony taking place at the Cenotaph on the usual lines with a special service in Westminster Abbey attended as in ordinary years by representative Service detachments.' His recommendation was acted upon, and could only be seen as a total victory for the people.

The Trafalgar Square meeting did go ahead as planned in 1923, though it was 'considerably revised and curtailed' and no longer featured the prime minister, who had withdrawn from the event. Billed as a National Call to Righteousness, and lasting for two hours, it was an experiment that was repeated in 1928 – as a Call to Peace – but never really caught on. Its chief, perhaps only, significance was that it was broadcast in its entirety by the British Broadcasting Company, founded just under a year earlier to provide radio transmissions to the nation. And the BBC would have its own role to play in cementing the structure of remembrance.

Over its first twelve months, the existence of the company had expanded radio listenership rapidly, so that it was estimated that the nightly audience was already around one million and still growing. The 11th of November 1923 was the first time that the BBC had the opportunity to mark Armistice Day, and it did so with the sounding of the Last Post, followed by the eleven o'clock chimes of Big Ben. Then, after the Silence, came

Reveille and 'O God, Our Help in Ages Past'. This was not how the Cenotaph service had been structured, and it was partly the BBC's endorsement of the Last Post that was to ensure the call was accepted as part of the central ritual of remembrance.

In subsequent years, the BBC made further encroachments on Armistice Day. In 1925 it broadcast an appeal by the Prince of Wales on behalf of the British Legion Fund, as well as a sermon by the Archbishop of Canterbury (doubtless cheering him when he praised the radio as 'the most striking of all the powers of science that compel or induce unity'), and the following year it transmitted a service from Canterbury Cathedral. Such broadcasts were well received, particularly in the remote parts of the country, such as Lundy Island in the Bristol Channel, where services were only held when a priest could be induced to travel out by boat. In other places, including Fremington in Devon, large numbers gathered to listen to the transmission as a communal act.

The real prize, though, would be to broadcast the Cenotaph ceremony itself, and the company's managing director, John Reith, began to lobby the government for permission so to do. Initially, he met with a complete rebuff, but he persevered and the tussle over the proposed transmission was to rumble on for several years.

At its heart was a clash not of principle but of practice, extending far beyond the act of remembrance. It was essentially a question of how the values and beliefs of society were transmitted, how the nation, this 'one big family', communicated with itself. The creation of Armistice Day provided a model example of the establishment at work, drawing on the contributions of the monarchy, the government, churches, civic authorities, newspapers and the military, as well as organisations such as the British Legion, the Boys' Brigade, the Boy

Scouts and the cadet forces. Each had a part to play in ensuring that the country came together as one.

The government therefore believed that the key to remembrance was the myriad of ceremonies throughout the country, which between them constituted a single, all-embracing service of national unity. Even if the Cenotaph were at the heart of that network, it should not be allowed to override local commemorations. In the words of Joynson-Hicks: 'It was felt that the whole idea underlying the Armistice Day services held throughout the United Kingdom is personal attendance by all who are able to be present.' By the time the BBC came into existence, the patchwork nature of the British state had again proved its worth. There had been problems surrounding remembrance in the immediate aftermath of war, but by the mid-1920s the riots and the demonstrations were mostly in the past, and the combination of decentralisation and participation that Joynson-Hicks was advocating had served its purpose in helping to calm the country. The complex lines of communication built over centuries appeared to be working perfectly, without the need for the startling innovation of broadcasting, and the intrusion of what the home secretary saw as 'mechanical contrivances', which were 'hardly appropriate to the spirit of the occasion'.

Seen from another perspective, the concept of Armistice Day could be taken as a prototype for the new world of the mass media. The idea of a single service replicated in thousands of locations simultaneously, in a network of shared meaning, was not dissimilar to radio itself, which promised that the whole country could participate in a communal experience whilst remaining in their own homes; geographic limitations could be transcended and the lines between public and private blurred. If the BBC were allowed to broadcast from the Cenotaph, it could effectively provide an alternative means of disseminating the culture of remembrance, and do so in what was potentially a much more reliable form. For the current practice depended on the presentation of common values, so that authority might speak with one voice, but there was always the danger that a pacifist priest or a socialist mayor might articulate dissent; the Cenotaph service, on the other hand, with the monarchy, the government and now the church in attendance, could always be counted upon to keep to the approved script.

As long, of course, as the BBC itself could be relied upon. And John Reith was anxious to prove its loyalty, as he demonstrated during the General Strike: 'Assuming,' he wrote to the prime minister, Stanley Baldwin, 'the BBC is for the people and that the government is for the people, it follows that the BBC must be for the government in this crisis.' From his point of view, if the broadcaster was ever to become accepted as the documenter of the nation, then the Cenotaph service was precisely the kind of thing it should be transmitting.

The argument was not put like that. Instead Reith insisted that the Cenotaph was the national monument and that the ceremony there was the national service; it was one to which all should have access, particularly those who would otherwise be denied participation at all. 'You state that identical services are available and that there are comparatively few unable to attend,' he wrote to the home office. 'I submit that there are hundreds of thousands of people who, however much minded, are prevented from participating in a local service, on considerations of time, infirmity, age, ill-health or simple distance.'

As letters to newspapers and politicians poured in, most of them supporting Reith's position, the government was again obliged to change its mind. 'The public demand for the broadcasting of the service is insistent,' conceded Joynson-Hicks in 1928; 'it is likely in my opinion to increase in volume and will eventually have to be met.' That 'eventually' did not prove to indicate a very long delay. The same year the BBC, having satisfied requirements that its equipment would not be too conspicuous, transmitted the Cenotaph service for the first time. As an acknowledgement of the profound significance of the occasion, broadcasting was then suspended, to allow for three hours of radio silence, until it resumed for the Trafalgar Square meeting.

Local services were affected by the broadcast, but not in any way that might be detrimental to the interests of the state; rather the message of the Cenotaph was reinforced. Many churches installed loudspeakers to transmit the programme and the recording was relayed abroad as far as New Zealand. 'The picture which the broadcast version of the ceremony at the Cenotaph gave to thousands of people in their homes and in churches throughout the country was quite a real one,' wrote *The Times*. Nor did fears of driving people away from local services materialise; some thirty thousand attended the Armistice Day ceremony in Portsmouth that year. Now vindicated, the BBC was to broadcast the Cenotaph service on radio every year, adding in 1937 television pictures to the sound.

The timing of that first transmission was fortuitous, for 1928 marked something of a turning-point in perceptions of the First World War. It was the year that Douglas Haig died, leaving behind in the British Legion an organisation that had become a byword for loyalty and patriotism. Haig's own reputation, which was to suffer grievously in the public mind in later years, was still intact at the time of his death, and he remained a popular figure.

Grieving women at an Armistice Day ceremony, some of them
wearing the medals of their dead menfolk

Thousands lined the streets as his funeral cortege – his coffin
carried on the same gun-carriage that had transported the
Unknown Warrior – made its way to Westminster Abbey, and
many more listened to the BBC's broadcast of the service,
which culminated in the Last Post and Reveille.

But this was also the year that saw the first production of
R.C. Sherriff's play *Journey's End*, set in the trenches, and the
publication of Edmund Blunden's *Undertones of War*, to be
followed in 1929 by a spate of books that similarly provided a
distinctly unglamorous account of the conflict: Robert
Graves's *Goodbye to All That*, Robert Aldington's *Death of a Hero*
and Ernest Hemingway's *A Farewell to Arms*, as well as the English
translation of Erich Maria Remarque's German classic *All
Quiet on the Western Front*. The last of these was advertised at

Christmas 1929 under the slogan: 'The Best Gift for the Season of Peace and Goodwill'. Meanwhile, although Rudyard Kipling remained the nation's best-known and most cherished poet, his star was beginning to wane, whilst the work of the war poets – Siegfried Sassoon, Wilfred Owen, Graves – was gaining wider currency.

In 1918 a letter received by the parents of a young British officer, shortly after they were told of their son's death, had been published in some newspapers, expressing what was then a commonly held view. 'Tomorrow at dawn there's a hell of a show coming off, and this will only reach you if I get knocked out,' the man had written, as he urged his family to be brave, adding: 'You'll be proud too, won't you? 'Cos it's the best death a chap can have.' Ten years on, such ideals of the honour and glory to be found in sacrifice still dominated the public expressions of remembrance, and still provided comfort and reassurance to many of the bereaved, but they were being challenged by other, ever louder, voices from amongst those who had served.

The changing tenor of the times was sufficient to provoke complaints from some quarters that the war poets should not be seen as representative of British soldiers. Certainly that was the argument of John Buchan, the great writer of imperial adventure stories. 'The vocal people were apt to be damaged sensitives, who were scarcely typical of the average man,' he wrote in his 1926 novel *The Dancing Floor*. 'There were horrors enough, God knows, but in most people's recollections these were overlaid by the fierce interest and excitement, even by the comedy of it.'

Nonetheless, the 'vocal people' were proving popular, despite some local attempts at censorship. When *All Quiet on the Western Front* was banned by the Port Sunlight Libraries

Committee, it was reported that 'The decision caused considerable controversy among the inhabitants of the village.' After a similar move was made in Rawtenstall, Lancashire, a petition by townspeople attracted over five hundred signatures. And in Ilkeston, Derbyshire, it took a full council meeting to agree that Remarque's novel might be bought for the town library. The genre was, moreover, a commercial success, with *Goodbye to All That* selling thirty thousand copies in its first few weeks. 'The sudden revival of the war book,' noted *The Times*, in its 1929 round-up of Christmas reading, 'took the book trade completely by surprise.'

British disquiet over this literature appeared mild and essentially democratic, however, when compared to reactions being expressed more forcefully, and much more ominously, elsewhere in Europe. The Italian government of Benito Mussolini banned a production of *Journey's End* and the publication of *All Quiet on the Western Front*, while in Berlin, screenings of the Oscar-winning adaptation of Remarque's novel were proscribed in 1930, following a vociferous and sometimes violent campaign led by the National Socialist Party and orchestrated by its leader in the city, Joseph Goebbels. In Britain, by contrast, the weight of the new institutions, particularly the British Legion and the BBC, was sufficient for the time being to contain the anti-war sentiment expressed in these works. The carefully constructed edifice of remembrance came with an inbuilt yearning to pursue peace; the notes of the Last Post seemed to promise 'Never again'.

Chapter Seven

STAND FAST

The Last Post calls; we hearken to its strain,
To stir within our hearts a boundless pride
For those who ventured, suffered, fought and died,
That liberty should be restored again.

Mollie Kremer
'The Last Post Calls' (1935)

There had been an expectation in the period immediately following the Armistice that the people would soon accept that this war, though different in scale from previous conflicts, was to be commemorated in much the same way. Certainly that had been the government's understanding, hence Alfred Mond's comment that there would be 'a demand for a greater and more imposing monument' than the Cenotaph, and Lord Curzon's belief that 'Armistice Day is not a day of national grief'. Hence too the comments of a civil servant named H.R. Boyd, as reported in the *Sunday Express* in 1926: 'The war has been over for eight years. It is time that sentiment gave way to common sense.' But a population that had been at least partially militarised saw things otherwise, and stubbornly insisted that the losses of the First World War were different not merely in quantity but also in quality from earlier hostilities.

In the 1930s the writer Arthur Mee coined the expression Thankful Village to refer to those places 'where all the men came back'. He could identify just twenty-three such villages, and though a later calculation was to find a further thirty parishes in the United Kingdom that had endured no losses, it was still a vanishingly small minority of communities. For all the rest, the task of commemorating the dead locally became part of a collective, national endeavour.

That first handful of civic war memorials listing the names of the dead in the Crimean War, amplified in the wake of the Boer War, now became the norm rather than the exception. In the first years of peace, war memorials sprang up in almost every village and town, as well as in the cities. Many were military, commemorating the dead of the great cavalry and infantry regiments and of the corps, adding to a long heritage of battle honours and regimental history; here it was still possible to see the First World War as an extension of a tradition of glory and pride. Others were also military, but belonged to the Pals battalions, standing to one side of the established institutions of the Army, a witness to the people's war. A great many others, however, were simply determined by location. Typical of many was Heavitree, a village on the outskirts of Exeter that had a population of just a few thousand; its memorial was unveiled on Easter Saturday, listing the names of 207 men and one Voluntary Aid Detachment nurse who had died, leaving behind sixty-five widows. In recognition that this was Holy Week, the unveiling was accompanied by the singing of the hymn 'On Resurrection Morning', after which buglers from the Royal Garrison Artillery sounded the Last Post.

Indeed, as the wave of memorials engulfed the land, the call of the Last Post was perhaps the only consistent element.

Everything else was subject to variation. Some monuments were religious in nature, others secular. Some were located in churchyards, others in the town square, others still in a place specially set aside. Some consisted of a simple cross, some an obelisk, and some a sculpture of a soldier, either alone or with ghostly comrades from the past or a grieving widow. Some bore inscriptions that spoke of victory, many of peace. Some even commemorated the enemy dead, as at Theberton, Suffolk, where the sixteen men killed when the German airship *L48* was shot down were remembered. And on top of Great Gable in the Lake District, nearly three thousand feet above sea level, was the highest war memorial in the country, a plaque commemorating the members of the Fell and Rock Climbing Club who had perished.

The blank expanse of the Cenotaph spoke in its silence for the entire nation, but many of these local monuments celebrated their own identities. In Snitterfield, Warwickshire, the names of thirty-five dead were recorded on a memorial, next to which was placed a seat bearing the inscription: 'The noble expanse visible from this spot was Shakespeare's favourite countryside. The men whose names are inscribed on the neighbouring monument gave their lives for that England which never did nor ever shall lie at the proud foot of a conqueror.'

There was almost endless debate about the form that a memorial should take, whether it should be a monument or something more utilitarian: 'a playground, a new cot or a new wing for a hospital, or even, as was suggested in one village, a weighing-machine for carts?' At the other end of the scale from such humble endeavours were the great civic monuments, such as the Glasgow War Memorial, unveiled by Douglas Haig in 1924, with a crowd of fifty thousand people in attendance.

The unveiling of the war memorial at Otham, near Maidstone in Kent, 1919

A similar process was under way throughout the Empire, again with significant local variations. In New Zealand, where there had been conscription during the war, the names of the dead were recorded; in Australia, where there had not, those named tended to be 'all who served, not just those who fell'.

And at every unveiling, there was one or more bugler or trumpeter, solemnly intoning the Last Post. Sometimes it was the cavalry call, but much more frequently — if there were no specific association with a cavalry regiment — it was that of the infantry, the piece that had been adopted by the nation as the most appropriate music for mourning the war-dead. It sounded in tribute to officers and other ranks, enemies and non-combatants without favour, and in its universality it articulated a democratic recognition that this had indeed been the people's war.

'All men are equal in death, whether friend or foe, rich or poor,' observed Colonel J.H. Chaballe of the Canadian Army in 1936. He was speaking on behalf of the Last Post Fund, an organisation founded in Montreal in 1909 by Arthur H.D. Hair to ensure that all servicemen received a proper funeral. So successful did the Fund become that by 1916 it was said that 'at the present time Montreal is the only part of the British Empire where an ex-soldier or an ex-sailor is certain of a decent burial owing to the activities of the society'. The Last Post Fund was subsequently launched too in Australia, where Sir Philip Game, former RAF air vice-marshal and governor of New South Wales, explained that it would 'with equal readiness extend the benefits of the fund to the soldiers, sailors and airmen of our allies and former enemies'. The fact that such an all-embracing venture was named after the Last Post was a recognition that the call had left behind its military origins, and now transcended divisions of class, religion and nation.

The same spirit was evident in the construction of war graves in Europe. There was some anger amongst the bereaved that no attempt was made to repatriate the bodies of the dead. 'I maintain that our dead belong to us,' insisted Sarah Ann Smith of Leeds; 'the government cannot stop us from having them removed if we wish.' She went on to found the British War Graves Association to campaign for the return of the bodies, but her endeavours were entirely unsuccessful. The scale of such an enterprise was considered too vast to be practical, and the alternative — of allowing those who could afford it to make their own private arrangements — too socially divisive.

Instead huge new cemeteries were to be laid out in what Rudyard Kipling called the 'largest bit of landscape gardening undertaken in any country'. In the discussions concerning this endeavour, Kipling, as a member of the Imperial War Graves Commission, was amongst those arguing for a uniformity of headstones, so that the wealthy could not outrank the poor in death, and that no distinction be made between officers and men. There must be no 'privilege in the face of death', he insisted, even though he was happy to concede: 'Lord knows I'm no democrat.' And so emerged the vast rows of graves, maintained by the Commission, with their identical, pristine white headstones – again, like the Cenotaph, a design intended to be non-denominational. Where the identity of the body could not be ascertained, the stone bore the inscription, chosen by Kipling: 'A soldier of the Great War. Known unto God.' The French equivalents had merely the single word: 'Inconnu'.

The erection of the war memorials in Britain and the creation of the cemeteries in northern Europe ensured that the mood of sombre remembrance lingered longer than the government had anticipated. 'It used to be said that the two minutes' silence could not be repeated for more than a few years,' noted the *Spectator* in 1927. 'By a wonderful and unforeseen evolution, however, the act of remembrance seems to have become more intense. The silence is more carefully organized by street crowds, who are barely aware that they are organizing it, and more scrupulously observed and felt.'

Almost every year the same observation was made, often with a note of wonder and a recognition that somehow the ceremony was being subtly transformed: 'Many prophesied that the Silence would die out with the passing of the years, but the annual scenes in cities, towns and villages are a striking proof of the hold Remembrance Day has on the world's heart.

Rudyard Kipling and King George V on a tour of war graves in
Northern Europe, 1922

What was originally a formal ceremony has now become an instinctive tribute.' Into the 1930s, there was still no sign of any decline. 'Each year one approaches the Armistice Day celebrations with an anticipation that the gatherings will be smaller than in the preceding year,' reported the *Manchester Guardian* in 1932. 'But today the throngs who met in the neighbourhood of the Cenotaph showed no diminution.'

The same report outlined the structure that had now been adopted at the Cenotaph. On the stroke of eleven o'clock, a gun was fired on Horse Guards Parade to signal the start of the Silence, with another to mark the end. Then 'the Royal Air Force buglers sounded the Last Post', there was the singing of 'O God, Our Help in Ages Past', and finally 'the buglers of the Royal Marines sounded the Reveille'. After the singing of the national anthem, the King departed, and the march past the Cenotaph began, 'which continued all day'.

That account, however, was not strictly accurate in two crucial respects. First, the Last Post was played by RAF trumpeters not buglers, and their use of cavalry trumpets to sound an infantry call made all the difference. Many years later, Lieutenant-Colonel C.H. 'Jiggs' Jaeger, director of music of the Irish Guards and himself a former bugle major, was to lobby for this to change, explaining: 'Last Post was composed essentially for the B flat bugle, and being of a different pitch it is a technical impossibility to perform this on the E flat trumpet unless certain modifications are made, which distorts the original melodic shape of the call.' As Jaeger's biographer, Colin Dean, pointed out: 'the call had to be played using the incorrect notes, something that had caused considerable comment and protest in the past as it sounded so wrong.' Jaeger was successful in his campaign, and from 1964 the Last Post was to be played on the instrument for which it had originally been written. But for four decades a mutilated version of the call had been sounded at the Cenotaph, in order to satisfy the need for ceremonial.

Furthermore, the Reveille played by the Royal Marine buglers was not the call of the same name that was familiar to anyone who served in the infantry. Rather it was the Naval Reveille, generally known as the Charlie Reveille, a much jauntier and shorter piece. At nearly a minute in length, the Army version, sometimes called the Long Reveille, was one of the more evocative and challenging calls in the repertoire, and although its absence made little difference to the general public, there were some old soldiers who were left feeling disgruntled. When a 1932 BBC broadcast from the Thiepval Memorial on the Somme included the Long Reveille, Lieutenant-Colonel P.R. Butler wrote to *The Times*, praising 'its sweeping and majestic cadences' and pleading for its reinstatement at the Cenotaph: 'There is only one call worthy – or so, I fancy, most soldiers think – to be sounded after Last Post and it is the beloved "old long Reveille" of the British infantry.' Twenty years later, the same correspondent was still making the same plea, though to little effect. When Jaeger's changes were implemented in 1964, the Marine buglers took over the sounding of the Last Post, and the RAF trumpeters ended the service with their own equivalent of Reveille, the Rouse. This pattern has continued.

As the format of the Cenotaph service stabilised in the early 1930s, other amendments were made to the rituals of Armistice Day. In 1934 the Westminster Abbey service added a new prayer for the disabled, as well as 'the singing of what has become almost a second national anthem, Blake's "Jerusalem", which typifies much of the spirit of the time'. The reason, explained a spokesman for the Abbey, was that

'As the years pass the nation naturally looks forward rather than backward to the past. People today are increasingly concerned with what can be done to advance those great ideals for which our people laid down their lives, and we have tried to reflect this in the Abbey service.'

In truth, there had always been an element of looking forward, a yearning for future peace. The order of service at the Abbey already suggested that the prayer during the Silence should be: 'In remembrance of those who made the great sacrifice, O God, make us better men and women and give peace in our time.' And as early as the first Silence in 1919, the more radical voice of the *Daily Herald* had spelt out an uncompromising editorial message: 'By the sacred memory of those lost to you, swear to yourself this day at eleven o'clock, that never again, God helping you, shall the peace and happiness of the world fall into the murderous hands of a few cynical old men.'

At that time too, there had been prayers offered in many churches for the newly founded League of Nations, the international organisation that – many believed – offered the best chance of keeping the peace, of preventing another conflict as bloody as the last war. David Lloyd George's attempt in 1919 to create a League of Nations Day on the 11th of November might not have materialised, but it did make some impression: all London County Council schools were instructed to follow the Silence that year with a lesson explaining what the League of Nations was and what it might do. That, of course, had been in the first flush of peace. By the early 1930s, the League's aspiration of avoiding future wars was looking ever more implausible. Germany and Japan withdrew as members in 1933, and two years later the Italian invasion of Abyssinia exposed the fundamental impotence of the organisation.

As fascism spread in Europe, and war clouds became once more visible on the horizon, the hope in Britain was that remembrance and peace might become two sides of the same coin. By the end of the 1920s, J.R. Clynes, home secretary in a Labour government, was acknowledging that the days of triumphalism were long gone. 'The purpose of the annual service at the cenotaph is I think universally regarded as a tribute primarily to the memory of those whose death the Cenotaph commemorates,' he remarked in a memo to the cabinet in 1929. He noted too that the presence of soldiers, sailors and airmen at the ceremony was proving controversial in some quarters: 'Some of my colleagues have no doubt received representations that the troops should be unarmed as a symbol of the nation's will to peace.'

Such thinking was not restricted to the Left. Armistice Day was 'really a peace celebration', suggested the *Catholic Times* in 1930, while the same year the *Daily Mail* recalled the old Roman proverb, *Si vis pacem, para bellum* (if you want peace, prepare for war), and updated it: 'if you wish for peace, remember war.' Not long after, the London County Council issued new guidelines to its schools about how to commemorate what it was now calling Armistice and Peace Day, whilst insisting that the message should not be confined to just this one day: 'peace teaching, if it is to attain its maximum effectiveness, ought to permeate much of the teaching of the ordinary subjects of the curriculum throughout the year'.

This was the spirit of the times that Westminster Abbey was seeking to harness, as it made adjustments to its service. 'Once again the people in countless cities, towns and villages of our empire have today heard the haunting notes of the Last Post,' editorialised the *Hull Daily Mail* in 1933. 'So long as Armistice Day is honoured, so long will people remember the futility and awful cost of war.' And, the paper felt obliged to insist, the presence of the military on such occasions did nothing to change that message: 'People who assert that the gatherings, parades and trumpet calls are an incentive to war are fools and worse.'

The fact that a mainstream newspaper was now talking of the 'futility' of war, rather than of its glory, was a sign of how the country had changed. It was a process that could be dated back to those first reports by W.H. Russell from the Crimea, revealing the reality of life in uniform. Later on, the Boer War, though widely supported, had stirred a vociferous anti-war minority in Britain to denounce the tactics used by the country's armed forces, protests that had not been in such evidence during previous conflicts. By the end of the 1920s, the realities of modern warfare being everywhere known in the aftermath of the trenches, it had become possible for a magazine like the *Spectator* to write: 'It is held almost universally now that war is a shameful thing, not indeed because it does not call out the noblest and bravest qualities of individual men, but because it is a disgraceful reflection upon the degree of reason at which civilized nations have arrived.'

The change was most evident not during the Armistice Day ceremonies themselves, so much as in what happened in the evening. In 1919 a memorial service had been held in St Paul's Cathedral for the fifty thousand former members of the Boys' Brigade who had lost their lives, and there had been other moments of solemnity up and down the country. For the most part, though, the evening of the first Armistice Day anniversary had witnessed scenes of joy and celebration: 'Every theatre in the West End was sold out, and all seats in restaurants were booked,' it was reported. 'A great Victory Ball was held in the Albert Hall. There were many regimental gatherings, also reunions of the WAACs, the Wrens, the Land

Girls and other war workers.' As the *Daily Sketch* put it: 'Quite frankly people wanted to dance.'

Two years later, the same still held true. 'In the morning there will be religious services and observances,' noted *The Times*; 'at night there will be revelry and song.' But the mood of rejoicing was gradually to be worn down by the twin forces of remembrance and economic hardship. 'Imperceptibly, the Feast-Day became a Fast Day,' regretted one veteran, 'and one could hardly go brawling on the Sabbath.' The ball at the Albert Hall, initiated in 1919, continued as an annual event, a fixed date in the social calendar of the upper class, but in 1923 it was preceded earlier in the evening, at the same venue, by a benefit concert in aid of the British Legion. This was a very different affair, featuring the premiere of a new symphonic work, *A World Requiem* by John Foulds (billed as 'a Cenotaph in sound'), performed by full orchestra, organ and a 1,200-strong Cenotaph Choir. 'Thousands were moved by the sublime music,' judged the *Daily Graphic*. 'For two hours and twenty minutes a non-musical audience sat enthralled.' Many more respected critics were less impressed.

It was in 1925 that the crunch came. It was announced that a Grand Armistice Night Ball would again be staged at the Albert Hall, this time in aid of the Royal Northern Hospital, with participants encouraged to attend in fancy dress and with dancing until four o'clock in the morning. 'Is it dreadfully old-fashioned to be shocked?' wondered Dick Sheppard, the vicar of St Martin-in-the-Fields, in a letter to *The Times*. 'A fancy dress ball on a vast scale as a tribute to the Great Deliverance which followed on the unspeakable agony of 1914–1918 seems to me not so much irreligious as indecent.'

His letter resonated with many others and attracted support from the likes of the *Daily Mail* ('it is better to keep Armistice

Night in the home than in the dancing hall') and Grace Joynson-Hicks, the wife of the home secretary: 'Personally, I would much sooner not have any sort of festivity on Armistice Day, for I think that the day should be kept quietly.' Many towns and cities around the country announced that they would not be issuing dancing licences for the evening of Armistice Day and, after several days of pressure, the organisers of the Albert Hall event conceded defeat: 'during the last week it has become apparent that a section of the community has a strong feeling against public rejoicing on Armistice Day.'

The ball was moved back to the 12th of November, leaving Armistice night free for a service to be held at the Albert Hall. Presided over by the Reverend Sheppard, it was comprised primarily of hymn singing, though the 'Hallelujah Chorus' was also performed and the Last Post and Reveille were sounded.

Thus ended the six-year run of Armistice Day balls. The following year, a new event, billed as a Festival of Remembrance, was inaugurated at the Albert Hall. That first Festival included a repeat performance of *A World Requiem* (its last ever performance), but thereafter — under the aegis of the British Legion — it began to take a shape that would become much more familiar. In 1927 the evening ended with the Prince of Wales leading the entire audience on a march to the Cenotaph, having made a speech in which he won loud cheers for his description of the war as one 'the like of which we pray God we may never endure again', and for saying: 'We can remember, too, that if we have a duty to the dead, we have also a duty to the living.' The real highlight of the evening, however, was when 'For fully an hour the audience, led by the band of the Grenadier Guards, sang old Army songs.' Broadcast on BBC radio, it was not only transmitted in Britain but relayed across the Empire, the first time this had been attempted, in a precursor of what was to become the BBC World Service.

The 1927 event set the tone for future Festivals of Remembrance, and by the end of the decade, all the key elements were in place. There was the Legion, there was royalty, and there was community singing of songs associated with the war years: 'Keep the Home Fires Burning', 'There's a Long, Long Trail', 'Take Me Back to Dear Old Blighty', 'It's a Long Way to Tipperary' and 'If You Were the Only Girl in the World'. There was too a religious element, expressed in the Act of Remembrance, the climactic section of the evening when the Silence, preceded by the Last Post and concluding with Reveille, was accompanied by a gentle blizzard of poppy petals, falling from the roof to cover the floor of the hall and the participants, one petal for each life that had been lost. The words of Laurence Binyon's 1914 poem 'For the Fallen' were spoken:

> They shall grow not old, as we that are left grow old:
> Age shall not weary them, nor the years condemn.
> At the going down of the sun and in the morning,
> We will remember them.

The dominant theme to emerge from the Festival was a celebration of comradeship, in tune with the intention of the British Legion's social clubs; it was a time when the audience 'could shout itself hoarse,' as it was reported in 1929, 'could cheer and cheer again, and crack the old jokes, and demand the repetition of this chorus or that'. This was not quite how Dick Sheppard had envisaged it turning out when he ended the fancy dress balls.

For the solemnity of the 1925 event, which he had largely shaped, had reflected Sheppard's own beliefs, and within a decade he was again writing to the newspapers with another, more controversial proposal. This time his letter to the *Manchester Guardian* suggested that British men should sign a pledge saying: 'We renounce war and never again directly or indirectly will we support or sanction another.' By now he was convinced that Christianity and pacifism were inseparable, and that both were essential to the survival of civilisation. 'No Christian man ought to touch war in any circumstances,' he argued, whilst also insisting: 'There is no alternative to Christianity.' In July 1935, and again on the 24th of May (Empire Day) in 1936, he was to be found back at the Albert Hall leading rallies for the pacifist movement he had founded and which became the Peace Pledge Union. By 1937 the PPU was staging an alternative gathering in Regent's Park on Armistice Day, where, 'instead of the customary bugle calls after the Silence, an anthem — "O Lovely Peace" — was sung by a choir of men and boys'.

The PPU also rejected that other great symbol of remembrance, the Flanders poppy. Instead it followed the lead of a section of the Co-operative Women's Guilds who, in 1933, had advocated the use of a white poppy, intended to symbolise peace and to be a remembrance of all who had died in the war, not just military combatants. The subsequent adoption of the white poppy by the more newsworthy PPU did not impress the British Legion, and when it was suggested that the Legion might wish to manufacture the new emblem, the proposal was angrily turned down. Nonetheless the white poppy did materialise, and in the late 1930s it was occasionally to be seen in Britain, sometimes on lapels and breasts, sometimes on wreaths that were laid on war memorials; the latter were, as often as not, immediately removed by, as one British Legion member put it, 'those who consider that a white poppy and a white feather stand for very much the same thing'.

The white poppy attracted considerable controversy, though it was never much more than a minor diversion. In 1937, the year that Sheppard died, some sixty thousand of the symbols were sold, at a time when the Legion could call upon six times that number of people merely to sell their tens of millions of Flanders poppies. In an era of dictators, of Hitler, Stalin, Mussolini and Franco, and with the memory of 1914–18 still so recent, the appeal of 'peace in our time' was obvious, and there was a deep desire not to become again involved in a Europe that was rapidly militarising. Even so, few in Britain were convinced of the practicality of pacifism. 'We believe as pacifists we have a different view of the Armistice and what Armistice Day commemorates than even the British Legion,' announced Canon Stuart Morris, Sheppard's successor as general secretary of the PPU, but there was no real rivalry of equals here.

And there was no challenge to the schedule that had now been fixed for Armistice Day. At the eleventh hour of the eleventh day of the eleventh month, ceremonies were held in churches and (more normally) at war memorials around the country, most now following the order set by the Cenotaph, which had become the national standard as soon as the BBC began broadcasting it: the Silence, the sounding of the Last Post, the laying of wreaths, a short service with prayers and 'O God, Our Help in Ages Past', the Reveille, and then a march past. And in the evening, the Festival of Remembrance at the Albert Hall, replicated by the British Legion in many towns and cities; a celebration which served – in a wider, metaphorical sense – as a national Reveille.

As the pieces finally fell into place, what was remarkable about the forms of remembrance that Britain had adopted was how diverse were their origins. The cast of characters who had constructed this national drama ranged from King George V,

Lord Haig and Sir Percy Fitzpatrick, through Edwin Lutyens and Rudyard Kipling, the creative geniuses of Empire, to those two troublesome priests, David Railton and Dick Sheppard, whilst John Reith had given it his stamp of approval. The resulting compromises, in a country that prided itself on evolution rather than revolution and that was still extending the democratic franchise, did much to ensure stability at a time when totalitarianism was descending on large parts of Europe, from Russia to Spain.

And at the heart of it all was the bugle call – attributable to no one – that had begun its transformation more than half a century earlier, spreading from the parade ground into military funerals and thence into the wider society.

Within the Army, the Last Post was still played nightly in army camps. It even became for some a symbol of defiant separation from the civilian society that had adopted their call. For despite the changed atmosphere of the 1920s, a certain pride was felt in some quarters that – with the end of conscription – the Army had been restored as a body of professional soldiers, men who again enjoyed their unique status as a breed apart. 'To us they were notes of pride, loneliness, ostracism, almost exile, for soldiers were considered the scum of society,' ex-soldier Spike Mays was later to write, as he recalled the Last Post being played by his friend Algy, an East End orphan who had once been a fairground boxer. 'The anthem was sounded. The square was silent. "Christ almighty!" said Trooper Pape, as he swallowed hard and went to rug up his gelding.'

The call, however, was no longer the exclusive property of the forces. In the years between the world wars, the Last Post became fixed not only as the accompaniment to remembrance, but as part of society, applicable far beyond its military origins.

It was played at the funeral of opera singer Dame Nellie Melba in 1931. It was played at the interment of five lead-miners killed in Youlgreave, Derbyshire, in 1932, and – by members of the Gresford Colliery Silver Band – at a memorial service to the 266 men killed in a 1934 pit explosion so devastating that only ten bodies were ever recovered. It was played by four buglers before the commencement of Arsenal's home match with Sheffield Wednesday in 1934, mourning the death a few hours earlier of the great football manager Herbert Chapman, and again at grounds around the country two years later to mark the death of George V, patron of the Football Association. It reached far across the political spectrum, so that it was played at a 1939 memorial meeting for the British members of the International Brigade who had died in the Spanish Civil War, and at a 1924 demonstration in Trafalgar Square by two thousand members of the British Union of Fascists; the latter was followed by a march past the Cenotaph, where wreaths were laid bearing the inscription: 'British Fascists – for King and Country'.

Beyond the Cenotaph, the most celebrated playing of the Last Post was to come not in Britain but in Belgium. In 1927 the BBC broadcast the unveiling of the Menin Gate in Ypres, a memorial that contained the inscribed names of tens of thousands of soldiers whose bodies had never been recovered or identified. It immediately began to attract visitors wishing to pay their respects to the dead, and for three months in the summer of 1928, and again the following summer, a ceremony was held each evening, at which the Last Post was sounded by buglers from the local fire brigade. The simplicity and understated power of the event proved sufficiently popular – some eighty thousand people signed the visitors' book in 1929 – that in 1930 it became a year-round observance, with the call

Over ten thousand British Legion members on a pilgrimage to
the Menin Gate, Ypres, 1928

being played at nine o'clock at night in the summer and eight
o'clock in the winter.

One of the earliest accounts, published in the *Spectator* in
August 1930, described those who gathered at the Gate:
'German as well as French tourists, and Belgian boys and
girls, and British from all the seas stand here together; some
of us pilgrims, some sightseers.' The ceremony itself was
commendably plain: 'Just before the clocks strike, two Belgian
policemen stop all traffic. We stand bareheaded. Buglers
come forward. Then the old call rings out against the arches
that bear the names of two hundred thousand of our dead.'
This, it was explained elsewhere, was a gift from the town to
the world: 'It is emphatically laid down that no British visitor

shall be asked to contribute towards the fund to pay the musicians and other incidental expenses, as the Yprois wish it to be their personal tribute to our Glorious Dead.' Nonetheless, the symbolism was such, and the gesture so appreciated, that donations were received, including four hundred pounds from the Surrey section of the British Legion in 1935.

Later in 1930 a similar nightly ceremony commenced at Loos, France, where there was another memorial to the missing. 'The Last Post will be sounded by one bugler — an ex-soldier in the employment of the Imperial War Graves Commission — beginning today, the fifteenth anniversary of the battle of Loos,' it was reported on the 25th of September. 'This is being done on the suggestion and at the request of the relatives of one of those commemorated on this memorial, who have provided for the additional expense involved for one period of twelve months.' The practice extended beyond that initial year, though, unlike the Menin Gate, the cemetery at Loos never became a major tourist attraction. Nonetheless, as with all other war-grave sites, it was a place of pilgrimage for the bereaved. 'It is a lonely little cemetery,' read a report in 1939, 'but its very simplicity makes it all the more touching and impressive.'

The benefactor who was funding the Last Post at Loos wished to remain anonymous, but by 1935 his identity had become known. On the memorial was listed the name of Lieutenant John Kipling of the Irish Guards, whose father Rudyard 'has announced his intention to ensure, as far as is humanly possible, by means of an endowment, that Last Post shall be sounded there for all time'. The poet's initial reticence was perhaps explained a few years later when it was reported of Loos that 'the Last Post is sounded every day at sundown in memory of Rudyard Kipling's son.' Such was Kipling's fame that his tribute to all the dead had become personalised to himself alone. Indeed so evocative was his name that his 1936 obituary in *The Times* wrongly claimed for him the better-known Ypres ceremony: 'Every night at the Menin Gate the Last Post is now sounded by the endowment of John Kipling's father.'

The nightly ceremonies at Ypres and Loos proved inspirational, and in 1931 a plan was announced that 'at sunset each evening the Last Post is to be sounded by British buglers at the seventeen memorials along the old battlefront to those British dead who have no known graves'. The proposal came from the British Legion, who estimated that a capital sum of five thousand two hundred pounds was required in order that 'Each memorial will have a British ex-service man as curator, on whom will fall the duty of sounding the Last Post.' The scheme was never implemented, and in any event the whole swathe of land on which the memorials stood was soon to be invaded in the course of another conflict.

After the arrival of German troops in Belgium in May 1940, the Menin Gate ceremony was transferred to Brookwood Military Cemetery in Surrey, where it was continued until the liberation of Ypres in 1944 allowed it to return home. The Last Post is still sounded nightly at the Menin Gate, though the ceremony at Loos ceased with the Second World War.

Chapter Eight

AS YOU WERE

There is a sound of bugles in the street;
The Last Post dies, and only echoes cling.
A silence falls upon the City's heart,
And people bow their heads, remembering.

J. Tyler
'Armistice Day' (1939)

On Saturday the 11th of November 1939, General Alan Brooke, the commander of II Corps of the British Expeditionary Force, found himself in northern France, where he attended an Armistice Day ceremony at the memorial to the dead of Vimy Ridge, a battle fought twenty-two years earlier. 'The white tall pillars of the monument standing out against the ashy grey sky seemed entirely detached from this earth,' he wrote, 'whilst the two red wreaths of poppies looked like two small drops of blood on that vast monument. They served as a vivid reminder of the floods of blood that had already been spilt on the very ground we were standing, and of the futility of again causing such bloodshed.' And then he gave an almost audible shrug: 'I suppose that it is through such punishments that we shall eventually learn to "love our neighbours as ourselves".'

The incongruity of remembering the dead of a world war barely two months after another had started was a common feeling that November. 'Year after year we stood in silence to honour the dead who had given their lives in the hope that victory over German militarism would put an end to war and open for Europe a new era of brotherhood and peace,' observed the *Yorkshire Post*. 'Now that we are again at war a painful sense of irony comes over us when we recall those hopes.'

'Mother and I sat still at eleven, but everyone else seemed to be carrying on with their activities,' wrote May Smith, a Derbyshire schoolteacher, in her diary. 'It does seem farcical to be celebrating the end of the last war while we're just at the beginning of a new one, which according to prophecy is going to make even the old one pale before it.' The meaning had changed. It was still important to mourn the dead, of course, but it was hard now to claim that the lives lost had achieved anything in their sacrifice, that it had been – as the Archbishop of Canterbury said in 1923 – a 'proud bereavement', let alone to believe that 'lest we forget' would lead inevitably to 'never again'. Many were beginning to ask: 'Why bother to celebrate Armistice Day, when its effects, as we have seen, are only temporary?'

This time round, there had been no attempt to build a volunteer army, and instead conscription for men aged between eighteen and forty-one was introduced immediately at the outbreak of war, on the 3rd of September 1939. Again the worlds of the soldier and the civilian were brought together, but now with renewed danger for those at home. Bombing raids on British cities had been a new development in the First World War; in this new conflict, everyone expected their return and anticipated, correctly, that they would be even more damaging and costly.

It was this expectation, rather than the weary feeling of repetition, that led to the cancellation of the Cenotaph service in 1939 and the announcement in most major cities and towns that no official Armistice Day ceremony would be staged; in an era of total war, to allow large crowds to gather in known places at a predetermined time was almost to invite attack by bomb and gas. Nor were people expected to observe the Silence publicly, but rather, as the official guidance suggested, 'in our hearts and homes'. Apart from anything else, all the usual ways of indicating its start – the maroons, sirens and artillery fire – had taken on once more their earlier associations: 'Owing to the risk of confusion with air raid warning, the signal will not be given for the Two Minutes Silence,' it was announced in Devon. Instead there were small, unofficial ceremonies. Typical was Weston-super-Mare, where the official service was cancelled, but the Last Post was still sounded at the war memorial in Grove Park.

Church services were, however, held in 1939. A Service of Remembrance and Rededication took place at Westminster Abbey and was transmitted on BBC radio, complete with the Silence, and similar services were held at St Paul's Cathedral and in churches throughout the nation. The Queen made a broadcast on the BBC and its overseas services to the women of the Empire, and several cinemas relayed the transmission live to packed audiences.

With official Armistice Day commemorations at war memorials suspended right through the Second World War, greater prominence was given to Remembrance Sunday. But the services had changed in nature: 'there was less of the pageantry of former days', and in addition to the reading of the Roll of Honour – the list of those who had died in the First World War – a new element was added in many churches, the reading of the names of those from the parish currently in uniform. The usual singing of 'O God, Our Help in Ages

Past' and 'O, Valiant Hearts' was augmented or replaced by the fearful 'For Those in Peril on the Sea', and by hymns with a more bellicose tone: 'Onward Christian Soldiers' and 'Fight the Good Fight'. Meanwhile, the sermons struggled to remain optimistic. 'Here we are in the midst of an even more bitter struggle,' observed the Reverend E.G. Goode of Felton, Northumberland, in 1944. 'What has gone wrong? Where have we failed? What is wrong with humanity?' The Last Post and Reveille were still sounded, though it was now just as likely to be by members of the Boy Scouts or the local cadet force, since so many men were serving overseas in uniform.

The temporary elevation of the padre over the bugler was not to last, however, and in many places congregations began to dwindle, just as they had in the First World War. 'Remembrance Day is scarcely observed this year, except for poppy-selling last weekend,' noted the church-going May Smith in 1941, while a correspondent to *The Times* lamented in 1944: 'Of late the numbers attending the places of worship on this day have been noticeably smaller than formerly.'

That Armistice Day of 1944 was to be the last of the Second World War, and Clara Milburn, a middle-class woman from Balsall Common, near Solihull, reflected on the changes since the end of the previous conflict. 'The one thing we did not foresee,' she wrote in her diary, 'was this chaotic world, this welter of destruction of life and property, this wholesale division of families. It is just as well we cannot see ahead – our hearts would break.'

The Festival of Remembrance at the Albert Hall was also suspended in 1939, though it was still staged elsewhere by local branches of the British Legion. The Nag's Head in Mickleover, Derbyshire, was the venue for one such event in 1940, with dancing until eleven o'clock in the evening, at which point buglers from the Sherwood Foresters sounded the Last Post: 'During the Silence, a hundred thousand poppy petals which had been hung from the ceiling in a Union Jack, were released in a shower.'

Primarily, though, the Last Post was heard in Britain during the Second World War not at commemorations, but at funerals, of which there were many more at home than there had been in 1914–18. It was sounded for veterans of the previous war, some of whom were now getting on in years; it was sounded for combatants in the current conflict who had been repatriated with wounds that were to cause their death; and it was sounded for many of the victims of the Luftwaffe's bombing campaign, including sixteen women of the Auxiliary Territorial Service, killed when their hostel in East Anglia was bombed, and buried in a communal grave, and at the mass funerals of those who died in the Coventry Blitz.

Elsewhere in the Empire, in countries that seemed – in the days before the 1942 bombing of Darwin – too remote for the enemy planes to reach, the commemorations continued on Armistice Day, on Empire Day and on other national days, often finding a renewed interest amongst the public. A crowd of thirty thousand gathered at the Cenotaph in Wellington, New Zealand, for Anzac Day in 1941, and two years later the same occasion attracted record attendances in Australia.

In Cape Town, and in some other South African cities, the custom of the daily two minutes' silence was revived, again signalled by the firing of the Noon Gun and ending with the sounding of the Last Post 'broadcast from many points in the city and some of the suburbs'. There was no exact equivalent in Britain, though on Armistice Day in 1940 the BBC announced that henceforth it would broadcast the chimes of Big Ben at nine o'clock every evening, followed by a minute of silence for those who 'would be glad in the national cause to have a minute set apart for consecration to the land they love and the success of its cause – as well as for thoughts of dear ones and for individual needs'.

The practice of honouring the enemy dead also continued from the First World War. In late 1939 the bodies of five German sailors washed up on the Kent coast and that of a German airman on Scottish shores. All were accorded appropriate funerals with coffins draped in swastika flags, volleys fired over the graves and the sounding of the Last Post. The following year, after a German bomber was shot down in south-east England, the crew were buried in a grave on which was placed a posy of flowers carrying the inscription: 'Perhaps someone's daddy – from two little girls.' Even as the bugler was playing the Last Post, the call was drowned out by the sounds of an aerial dogfight above. There were, though, some who felt this was all going too far, and when four Luftwaffe airmen were shot down in a Heinkel in 1941 and given the same reverential treatment, the *Spectator* made its voice heard: 'If it is a choice between honouring and dishonouring Nazi airmen, let it by all means be the former, but a middle course – decent private interment – seems to fit the case better.'

Such practices were, however, reciprocated, at least in prisoner-of-war camps. Jimmy Howe, a bandsman in the Royal Scots who had been captured in France in 1940, spent most of the war in Stalag 8B, where he put together a dance band, playing instruments donated by the Red Cross or bartered from the German guards. When his drummer, Joe Edgar, died in 1942, 'He was given a military funeral in the large cemetery near the Stalag, with the band playing at his graveside and a guard of German soldiers who fired a volley in tribute.' Other prisoners of war had also acquired instruments, and in 1944 it was reported that Anzac Day had been marked by some nine hundred Australian and New Zealand troops in Stalag 383: 'the Last Post was sounded by five buglers, two minutes' silence observed, and Reveille sounded.' Even in the Japanese prison camps, there were some instruments to be found. Wally Granland, of the Australian Imperial Force (AIF), had a bugle with him when he was interned in Changi in Singapore, and – in a camp where some eight hundred and fifty died – was frequently called upon to sound the Last Post.

Conditions for funerals were scarcely better in theatres of war. 'Day after day living men of the AIF have gathered their dead comrades from the battlefields and brought them here to a simple burial and makeshift memorials,' it was reported, in the aftermath of the second battle of El Alamein in 1942. 'Australians mixing cement for headstones close by, and men from other units, down tools for a moment and stand to attention, joining in the simple familiar hymns with hushed voices. Then the Last Post, with its utter finality and long echoes over the sandhills, a brief inarticulate pause, and work starts again on the headstones and cement.'

Still the old call retained its transcendent symbolic power. On Armistice Day in 1944, as Allied troops continued to drive the German forces back, the British prime minister Winston Churchill and General Charles de Gaulle, the leader of the Free French Forces, stood to attention at the Tomb of the Unknown Soldier under the Arc de Triomphe, and the Last Post rang out in newly liberated Paris.

By the time that Japan signed a document of surrender on the 2nd of September 1945, Britain had been at war for just a day short of six years. The numbers of Empire dead were lower than in the First World War, but still far in excess of any other conflict, and the number of British civilians killed was considerably higher than in 1914–18. (Then there had been around fifteen hundred British fatalities as a result of enemy raids; now that figure exceeded forty thousand.) It had long been apparent that, when peace finally came and the official commemorations of remembrance were resumed, there would have to be changes to recognise this new struggle.

Shortly after VE Day on the 8th of May 1945, leaders of various churches, together with representatives of the British Legion, met Herbert Morrison, the home secretary in the wartime coalition government, to discuss the form that national remembrance should take once hostilities were concluded. Their view was that a single day should be chosen 'in commemoration of two national deliverances and of the fallen in both of the wars'. This, they argued, should not be the 11th of November, partly because of 'the uncertainty of the weather' and partly – a somewhat obscure note – because it tended 'to collide with Civic Sunday, which follows the election of new mayors'. Instead, they proposed that some time in May might be appropriate, and Morrison seemed sympathetic to their view, being personally inclined towards VE Day itself.

As the coalition dissolved, it fell to Morrison's successor, Donald Somervell, to bring the matter to cabinet. With no certainty that the war with Japan would be finished by November, he proposed that for this first year, the commemoration of Armistice Day should continue, a decision made easier because in 1945 it fell on a Sunday. The final decision could then be put off until the following year.

And so, for what was assumed in official circles to be the last time, the Cenotaph again became the focus of the nation's

Crowds gather at the Cenotaph on VE Day, the 8th of May 1945

thoughts on the eleventh hour of the eleventh day of the eleventh month. King George VI, accompanied by his daughter Princess Elizabeth in her Auxiliary Territorial Service uniform, joined large crowds for 'the sudden well-remembered stillness', and laid wreaths on the monument. It was noted, however, that in some cities and towns, the numbers of those attending were not quite what they had been in the 1920s and 1930s.

It was a world in which peace seemed scarcely sustainable, despite all attempts at reconciliation. In Berlin, it was reported, Germans commemorated the day for the first time, alongside the troops of the occupying Allied armies, and in Jerusalem, Arabs and Jews attended a service in a British military cemetery, where prayers were offered for the future of Palestine. But in Washington, the newly elected British prime minister, Clement Attlee, joined the American president Harry S. Truman and Canadian prime minister Mackenzie King to lay wreaths on the Tomb of the Unknown Soldier 'before boarding the Navy yacht *Sequoia* to discuss the atom bomb and other grave problems'. In 1919 the first Silence had been staged against an international backdrop of the Bolshevik revolution and British involvement in the Russian Civil War; now it was held in the shadow of the mushroom clouds over Hiroshima and Nagasaki. As one Australian newspaper wrote of the leaders of the free world: 'They are afraid of a third and worse world war, which almost inevitably would mean the end of civilisation as mankind now knows it.'

Over the next few months, as the British government began the process of reconstruction, it also took further soundings about how the war should be commemorated. The conclusion was that there was little need for change, that the structure of remembrance that had evolved in the years after 1918 – largely shaped by the people's will – still addressed the nation's needs, that there was no reason to dispense with the Silence, the Poppy, the Cenotaph or the Last Post and Reveille. The only difference would be the day on which it all happened.

Various options were considered, including VE Day, VJ Day and Battle of Britain Day, as well as less plausible candidates such as the 15th of June (to commemorate the signing of the Magna Carta) and the 14th of August (the signing of the Atlantic Charter), before it was decided to go for the minimum disruption, both at home and in the Empire and Commonwealth. In 1946 Attlee announced to the House of Commons that Armistice Day would be replaced by Remembrance Day, to be held on the Sunday before the 11th of

November (except when the 11th or the 12th fell on the Sunday). This would now be the national day of remembrance for the dead of both world wars. 'The Two Minutes Silence, that most pregnant of any corporate act devised in our time, will for the future be observed on Remembrance Day,' explained *The Times*. 'There will thus be no Silence next Monday.'

On the first Remembrance Day, in 1946, George VI, like his father before him, again unveiled the Cenotaph, onto which had now been added the dates of the Second World War. Henceforth it was the Sunday, not Armistice Day, that would be known as Poppy Day.

One other change was made, a subtle re-ordering of events. The Festival of Remembrance, previously staged on the evening of Armistice Day, was in 1945 moved to the Saturday evening before Remembrance Day, where it was to remain. The old idea of mourning the dead and then celebrating comradeship was reversed, thereby losing some of its old symbolic power of survival and rebirth. But an element of the community singing was instead brought into the Cenotaph service itself; where military bands had once played 'folksongs and laments' to accompany the march past of serving personnel and veterans, they now played music from popular songs of the two wars. Meanwhile, the shower of poppy petals at the Festival was increased in number to reflect the newly swollen ranks of the dead.

Although no attempt was made to produce a national memorial to stand alongside the Cenotaph, the tradition of local monuments was extended. Some simply had a plaque added, bearing a further list of the dead, but new memorials were also erected over the next few years, many of them dedicated to the RAF, whose contribution to the Second World War had proved so vital and so inspiring. One such was the stone in Sturminster Marshall, a village of eight hundred people in Dorset, unveiled in 1945 by the children 'of Albert Collins, a Naval stoker, who was among the local men who made the supreme sacrifice during the recent war'.

Even so, it couldn't feel the same as it had in the 1920s. The new Remembrance Day was accepted by the public, and was suitably marked around the country, but it would never grip the national imagination in the way that the old Armistice Day had done. Something had been lost along the way, and possibly it was the element of faith in the future, the hope that the world would never again see slaughter on such a scale. Some continued to mark the Silence privately on Armistice Day, but their thoughts were often fearful. In November 1939 a Mass-Observation researcher had noted a forty-year-old working-class man saying that he might as well buy three poppies: 'one for 1914, one for this war and one for the next'. Nothing that happened in the ensuing six years did much to dispel such anxieties. 'If anyone had told me on 11 November 1918,' wrote an Edinburgh antiques dealer in his Mass-Observation diary, 'that, twenty-nine years later, I should observe the Silence in my kitchen, with two German POWs from World War II, I should have thought they were crazy. I wonder with whom I shall observe it in, say, ten years' time, after World War III has happened.'

The public commemorations also failed to inspire the near-total observation they had once commanded. In 1948, torrential rain meant that only five thousand or so turned out to witness the Cenotaph service, and it was noted that there were many who did not even lower their umbrellas as a mark of respect during the Silence, preferring to remain dry. Two decades earlier, such weather conditions would not have deterred the crowds. The same year the Silence in Manchester 'was not unmarred; other chimes broke into it and traffic noises reduced its intensity'. After the wreath-laying, 'Last Post reached out once more far into the streets, where some of the passers-by paused to honour it while others went unmoved about their business'. By the next decade the reports were becoming somewhat defensive. 'The fact that there were only about five hundred people at the borough war memorial on Shepherds Bush Green made no difference to the way they felt,' insisted the *West London Observer* in 1954. 'They were secure in the knowledge that at eleven o'clock precisely they would be joined in their prayers by kindred souls all over Britain.'

A similar experience was noted elsewhere in the Empire. On the first Remembrance Day in 1946, fewer than five hundred attended the Cenotaph ceremony in Sydney, and in Brisbane there were fewer than a hundred: 'They stood with heads bowed. Many women were weeping. But traffic moved freely in nearby streets and even the sounding of Last Post and Reveille failed to halt pedestrians in Anzac Square.'

There were also criticisms of the British Legion to be heard in those post-war years. 'I have no time for all this Legion annual nonsense,' observed a Sheffield housewife on Armistice Day in 1945; 'if ever a body was corrupt, the British Legion is the one. More than time it was investigated and exposed and finished.'

The man who attempted to do just that was Harry Pursey, who had served in the Royal Navy during the First World War and had been elected as the Labour MP for Hull East in 1945. He publicly criticised the Legion's plush headquarters in Pall Mall, complained that the senior officials were overpaid, and suggested that there should be only one charity for ex-servicemen, supported by profits from the NAAFI. His most serious line of attack was on the selling of poppies ('this national cadging by tin-rattling'), describing it as 'the greatest charitable scandal of the century', and claiming that more than 25 per cent of the money raised was spent in expenses. The Legion responded with a booklet itemising the accounts of the organisation, which revealed that the manufacture of the poppies took up a surprisingly high 8.6 per cent of its expenditure. It was argued, however, that this was justified since the poppy factory provided work for 369 badly disabled ex-soldiers. Pursey retorted that the men were paid less than the average wage of a manual worker.

At the heart of the dispute was a clash of values. Many of those who voted in the Labour government in the landslide election of 1945 had done so with the memory of the 1920s uppermost in their minds. There was a determination to remedy the failure in that decade to build 'a land fit for heroes', and the new administration concentrated much of its effort on changing the nature of society in a way that David Lloyd George's government had never done. The centrepiece of this endeavour was the creation of the welfare state, as outlined in the report published in 1942 by a committee headed by William Beveridge. It was a task to which the new prime minister had a personal commitment. Having served right through the First World War, Clement Attlee had returned to fight poverty in the East End of London. He had outlined his thoughts on social provision in his first book, *The Social Worker* (1920), writing of 'the utter failure of charity to cope with the difficult problems of poverty', calling for 'collective rather than individual action', and quoting William Blake's lines about Jerusalem in England's green and pleasant land.

That last image, of building a new Jerusalem, was to become attached to the Labour government as it began to implement Beveridge's recommendations. In a socialist society, it was believed, none should be abandoned to the vagaries of the voluntary sector; the relief of temporary hardship should instead fall within the remit of the state. The endeavour was successful enough that this time there were no demonstrations by ex-servicemen; the limits of its achievement, however, were apparent in the dispute over the British Legion.

For while Harry Pursey insisted that there was no need 'for Legion charity in a Welfare State', the cultivation of the charitable instinct was precisely what Douglas Haig had been aiming at from the very birth of the organisation. 'The Legion is based on ideals of personal service which impel thousands of men and women to give up a large amount of their leisure in order to work for the cause,' protested William Keil, a member of the Buxton branch. 'Is then this ideal of service before self to be discarded and replaced by the typical regimented system which we know already?' The argument was essentially over the role and extent of the state as opposed to the individual, and it was won comprehensively by the Legion. Few were prepared publicly to back Pursey's campaign, and the Legion continued to tap into the enormous wellspring of public goodwill.

That goodwill extended to all aspects of remembrance, even if it was increasingly a passive support. And underneath the gradual decline in remembrance, there was a slow change in public attitudes, partly determined by the fact that little new had been introduced after the Second World War; that the existing forms of remembrance were merely extended to incorporate the more recent conflict.

The public perception of the Nazi regime had been set by the experience of the Blitz, during which period Britain had suffered more civilian than military fatalities; it had then been hardened by the terrible revelations of the concentration and death camps. The actions of the Third Reich were thus

seen to be of an entirely different order from those of the
Kaiser's Germany, and the subsequent understanding of the
ideology underpinning Britain's involvement in the two wars
was correspondingly different: one was political, an attempt
to curb German imperialism; the other was moral, a battle
against evil. Yet the two conflicts were linked, not only by
name but also now by remembrance, and that link prompted
a search for common factors. There were two to be found:
first, a suspicion of Germany in particular and of Europe in
general, and second, the scale of the killing. Both were to
help shape Britain for the rest of the century and beyond.
The former reinforced a longstanding distrust of the
Continent and of involvement in European politics; the
latter fed into a turn away from Britain's military heritage and
a growing aversion to war.

This second development was sometimes, but rarely,
manifest as outright pacifism. Mostly it was a case of seeing
war in terms of the human cost, rather than of objectives
achieved; certainly the talk of glory and triumph, so prevalent
in the popular literature of late-Victorian and Edwardian
Britain, was now much rarer. Instead there was a wave of films
about the war, such as *The Dam Busters* (1955) and *Reach for the Sky*
(1956), and about prisoner-of-war camps, *The Wooden Horse*
(1950) and *Bridge on the River Kwai* (1957), that centred on the
resilience and quiet heroism of individuals. There had been
no equivalent in the 1920s, and not simply because the British
film industry of that time was less developed. The First World
War had then been perceived in precisely the terms that the
Attlee government was later to extol: as a collective enterprise
rather than as atomised actions. But the war movies of the
1950s were made at a time when the national culture was
rejecting Attlee's vision. The period of austerity that followed

the return of peace had preserved some semblance of national unity, but the end of rationing in 1954 symbolised a new era, when individualism would come to eclipse community, and British cinema reflected this shift in attitude.

Furthermore, these films, accompanied by books, comics and toys, began to construct a creation myth for modern Britain, helping to foster a conviction that the country had indeed experienced the 'finest hour' of which Winston Churchill had spoken. Since the evil of Nazism was so clear and so total, the Second World War was understood in the public culture as a deeply regrettable but necessary struggle; it had been a just war, a good war, a war that had defined Britain's place on the moral high ground. A country that had virtually bankrupted itself, that had lost its political pre-eminence, that was witnessing the collapse of its Empire, could at least draw comfort from the belief that the sacrifice had been made for the good of humanity. On the occasion of the fortieth anniversary of VE Day, the Archbishop of Canterbury, Robert Runcie (who had been awarded the Military Cross during the war), was to preach a sermon in which he reflected: 'The victory which closed down Belsen, Buchenwald and Auschwitz is in itself sufficient cause for thanksgiving.' This, of course, had not been the motivation for Britain's declaration of war in 1939 – indeed, only one of those three camps had then been in existence – but it had become necessary to Britain's self-identity to place the emphasis here.

One consequence of a moral interpretation of the Second World War was that it subtly changed feelings about 1914–18. The growing antipathy to armed conflict began to colour popular perception of the earlier hostilities, and the First World War was increasingly to be seen simply in terms of slaughter. As memories faded, so too did the voices justifying

British war aims in 1914, until all that was left was an awareness of the numbers of dead, visible on the monuments in every town centre and every country church, but now with an addendum of yet more names.

The word 'sacrifice' that had been so prevalent in the 1920s and '30s was seldom, in later years, to be applied to the First World War, or if it were, it was qualified by an adjective: 'senseless' or 'tragic' or 'futile'. The dispute over how 1914–18 was to be interpreted had been resolved in favour of the war poets: the stark horror of Wilfred Owen's work was becoming more widely read than Rudyard Kipling's poetry of martyrdom and patriotism. And remembrance itself played its part in that transformation, with its emphasis on loss rather than victory.

Over time, the symbols of remembrance themselves would be annexed in a new cause. In 1969 the image of the vast rows of headstones, stretching as far as the eye could see, in places like the Tyne Cot Cemetery at Passchendaele, found a resonant cultural counterpart in the closing scene of *Oh! What a Lovely War*; Richard Attenborough's film of the radical, anti-war musical ended with an aerial shot of thousands of white crosses on the South Downs, filling the entire screen, no matter how far the camera pulled back or panned. Both images inspired sorrow and pity, but the reverence of Passchendaele was being replaced in the public mind by the anger of the latter. Grief does not cascade down the generations; bitterness and resentment sometimes do.

At around the same time, Tony Richardson's film *The Charge of the Light Brigade* (1968) revisited the subject of Tennyson's most famous poem and focused not on the heroism but on the blundering of hedonistic, incompetent aristocrats, on the donkeys rather than the lions. Meanwhile

George MacDonald Fraser launched his series of books about the villain from Thomas Hughes's Victorian novel *Tom Brown's School Days* with *Flashman* (1969); in this, and in subsequent novels, the much-vaunted valour and honour of the Empire were held up to comic ridicule. Even rock music was to make its contribution, with the first two concept albums by British bands – the Pretty Things' *S.F. Sorrow* (1968) and the Who's *Tommy* (1969) – both addressing the traumatic impact on their title characters of the First World War; neither evoked a vision of noble sacrifice.

This recasting of British history was to become most evident in the 1960s, but its seeds were there in the late 1940s. Even then, there seemed somehow a note of weariness about the old rituals, as compared to the experiences of a quarter of a century earlier. Perhaps there was also a sense of bathos. On the one hand peace had brought the proud restoration of the nightly sounding of the Last Post at the Menin Gate, but there was too the story of Harry Aldiss, a merchant tailor from Cambridge, who died in 1946. In his will he left a hundred pounds to Cambridge Borough Cemetery, 'the income to pay £1 to a trumpeter or bugler of the Regular or Territorial Army for sounding Reveille and Last Post at my graveside at twelve noon on my birthday, October 4, each year, and then saying: "Do your best for England".' It wasn't a very inspiring rallying-cry.

Chapter Nine

DISMISS

Did they beat the drum slowly?
Did they sound the fife lowly?
Did the rifles fire o'er ye as they lowered you down?
Did the bugles sound the Last Post in chorus?
Did the pipes play the Flowers of the Forest?

Eric Bogle

'No Man's Land' (1976)

On the evening of the 14th of August 1947 the time-honoured ritual was staged again. The soldier put the bugle to his lips and began to play the unmistakeable strains of the Last Post, whilst other soldiers stood to attention, their eyes fixed on the flagstaff, where the Union flag fluttered in the warm breeze. As the final notes of the call died away, the men saluted and the standard was lowered. The ceremony had been staged countless times before, unvarying in its repetition. The only difference on this occasion was that the flag would not be raised again the next morning. For this was India, and tomorrow India would cease to be part of the British Empire and would instead become an independent nation.

It was to become a familiar scene over the next few decades. Time and again, in former colony after former colony, as the Empire finally dismantled itself, the Last Post sounded in mourning not for an individual but for the history of the nation. The call was even played by former colonies as they themselves withdrew from their conquests; in 1990 the South African president F.W. de Klerk attended a ceremony in Windhoek where the Last Post was sounded as the South African flag was lowered and Namibia officially became an independent state.

It was enough to quicken the pulse of even the most self-consciously post-imperial Briton. In 1997, as the bugle played the Last Post at the handover of Hong Kong to China, the prime minister Tony Blair noted: 'I still felt a tug, not of regret but of nostalgia for the old British Empire.' That particular departure had been a long time in preparation and was accomplished with carefully choreographed ceremony. Others were not always staged with as much dignity as might have been wished. In 1976 the last British soldier left Singapore after more than a hundred and fifty years of the Army's presence, 'and for the final lowering of the Union Jack they even had to borrow a bugler from Singapore's Gurkha Presidential Guard'.

The evolution of the British Empire into the Common-wealth of Nations sparked much concerned debate about the legacy of imperialism, about what had been left behind that might be considered to be of positive benefit. Not always much noticed in that legacy was the Last Post, and yet it survived and thrived almost everywhere it had travelled, in the most unlikely of circumstances. The year after Indian independence, the country was brought to a shocked standstill by the murder of its spiritual father, Mohandas Gandhi, a man who had devoted his life to the struggle for freedom from Britain and to the philosophy of non-violence. Yet, as a million people gathered to witness the immersion of his ashes in the waters at the sacred confluence of the Ganges and Yamuna rivers, there seemed nothing incongruous in the ceremony's accompaniment by trumpeters sounding the Last Post, the music that had once belonged exclusively to the British Army. Nor that, nearly four decades later, at the funeral of his namesake Indira Gandhi, two dozen buglers should again sound the call as her son, Rajiv, walked seven times around her bier carrying a torch, before setting light to the kindling.

Virtually all of the military music bequeathed to India by the British Army was gradually to be replaced by Indian tunes – though 'Abide with Me' and 'Auld Lang Syne' remained in use – but there was no attempt to supplant the greatest of the bugle calls. 'The Last Post followed by the Reveille, played by buglers for a fallen soldier, still continue to stir emotions as deeply as in colonial days,' an observer noted in 1984. The Last Post is still sounded on Republic Day in India. Similarly it is still played on Independence Day and on Martyred Intellectuals Day in neighbouring Bangladesh.

Most extraordinarily of all, it continued to be played on both sides of the border between India and Pakistan in Punjab, the scene of so much conflict over the decades. 'For fifty-odd years, barring the occasional war,' it was reported in 1998, 'soldiers of the two countries have ceremonially raised and then lowered their respective flags at dawn and at dusk.' Every day, at sunset, rival versions of the call were to be heard on opposite sides of the divide. 'It is so ironic,' one Indian remarked. 'After more than fifty years of independence the only thing we seem to be able to co-operate on is when to blow the Last Post.'

Or perhaps that wasn't so extraordinary. For there was a long tradition of the call's use by both sides in a conflict, and of its adoption by those who were, in all other respects, dedicated to fighting British rule. In the aftermath of the 1916 Easter Rising in Dublin, Thomas Ashe, one of the Irish republican leaders, died after being force-fed during a hunger strike in jail, and was given a military funeral: 'his comrades have donned the forbidden uniforms; the forbidden rifles have been resurrected to fire a salute; the Last Post is to ring in Glasnevin Cemetery'. It rang again in 1923 to dedicate the cenotaph that had been erected at Leinster House, the seat of government of the Irish Free State, in memory of Arthur Griffith and Michael Collins and it rang again every August in an annual ceremony at the monument.

It continued to be played by all sides in the Troubles in the 1970s and 1980s, by the British Army, by the Loyalist paramilitary groups – at, for example, the funeral of murdered UDA leader Tommy Herron in 1973 – and by their Republican counterparts, as at the 1981 funeral of IRA hunger striker Bobby Sands. In 1976 ten thousand people gathered in Milltown Cemetery in Belfast to mark the sixtieth anniversary of the Easter Rising: 'Messages of solidarity from groups of Provisional IRA prisoners, both men and women, were read out, a volley of shots was fired over the Republican plot, and a bugler sounded the Last Post.'

Once, the Last Post had sounded around the world as a symbol of Empire; then it sang the epitaph to Empire; and finally it lived on, even after the imperial waters had receded, in almost every nation that had been touched by Empire. It was played at the funeral of Nelson Mandela in South Africa in 2013, and it was heard frequently in Robert Mugabe's Zimbabwe. Indeed it had been played at the birth of Zimbabwe, in yet another ceremony of decolonisation in 1980, a black bugler sounding the call as a white police officer lowered the flag in the presence of Prince Charles and the departing Governor of Southern Rhodesia, Winston Churchill's son-in-law Lord Soames. Even in those places where it was not officially adopted after independence, it was still to be heard. There was some concern in Hong Kong about whether the traditional Remembrance Day commemoration would be allowed to continue under Chinese rule; it did so unofficially at the existing war memorial, where a lone bugler played the Last Post to mark the end of the Silence. Meanwhile a state-sponsored event was being planned for the following year, 'designed as a memorial service to the dead of all wars, not just those that were important to Britain'.

Neither was the practice confined to the former Empire, for much of Europe also took it up. The exporting of the call had begun early, during the Peninsular War, when General William Beresford, in his capacity as a marshal in their army, had introduced the Last Post to the Portuguese. In the 1930s France created its own call, Aux Morts, but until that point the French Army had borrowed those of others. After the American entry into the First World War, Taps became popular ('I'd like to be minister of war for just five minutes so I could order Taps as our own official salute,' a French general commented) but for major state funerals, including those of Marshal Joseph Joffre in 1931 and even as late as that of General Philippe Leclerc in 1947, it was the Last Post that was played.

Belgium too adopted the Last Post as its own, and the call was sounded at the funeral of King Albert in 1934. From there it spread to Belgian colonies, including the Democratic Republic of the Congo (later renamed Zaire). In 1966, Joseph-Desiré Mobutu, the country's brutal dictator, had four former cabinet ministers publicly executed in front of a crowd of eighty thousand, having declared a national holiday to celebrate the occasion; as each of the condemned men was led to the scaffold, four buglers sounded the Last Post. The grisly ceremony carried echoes of more barbaric times in Britain. Nearly three centuries earlier, in the aftermath of the battle of Sedgemoor, which ended the Duke of Monmouth's rebellion against James II, Colonel Percy Kirke had nineteen of the rebels hanged; seeing their bodies shake in their death throes, it was said that he declared he would give them music to dance to, and ordered his drummers and trumpeters to strike up lively airs.

Beyond all these official uses, the Last Post had become part of the cultural vocabulary of Britain. It was frequently to be heard in an ironic context at sporting occasions, played by individuals in the crowd, as, for example, when Spurs lost 4–0 to Arsenal in 1967, or when England lost to Australia in the third Ashes Test at Melbourne in 1979. It was sounded daily in the Duke of York pub in Charlotte Place, London – one of novelist Anthony Burgess's favourite haunts – where the landlord, Major Alf Klein, kept a bugle behind the bar and sounded the call at closing time every night. It was performed when the liner *Aquitania* left Southampton on its last voyage to a breaker's yard in 1950; when the Waveney Valley railway line between Beccles, Suffolk, and Tivetshall, Norfolk, was closed down in 1953; and when the Old Vic theatre closed (temporarily, as it turned out) in 1981.

Conversely, however, the daily routine of the bugle call was dropping out of use in the Army. It had survived into the modern world, but by the end of the 1960s the everyday calls were becoming less familiar. For some, the final blow came in 1970 when the defence secretary, Denis Healey, scrapped the old Army system of low basic pay combined with complicated allowances for food and lodging, and replaced it with the 'military wage', introducing a substantial pay rise at the same time. It was now assumed that even the lowliest of soldiers could afford to buy a watch. The Last Post continued, and continues still, to be sounded nightly in the Ceremony of the

Keys at the Tower of London, but nowhere else in the British Army is it still used in its original context, to announce that the camp has been secured for the night.

As that old function faded in the post-war years, new settings for the Last Post were appearing. In 1939 Hector Adkins, the director of music at Kneller Hall, had introduced a version of the call accompanied by timpani, 'conveying a Wagnerian impression of dignity and solemnity'. That version didn't catch on, but later the same year, at the Aldershot Tattoo in July, as war was becoming inevitable, Owen Geary of the Royal Artillery produced an arrangement of the Cenotaph hymn 'O God, Our Help in Ages Past', with the Last Post ringing out on trumpets above the melody. In the post-war years this combination of the call with various hymn tunes became common at services and tattoos: 'Abide with Me', 'Lead, Kindly Light', 'The Day Thou Gavest Lord Is Over', even 'Auld Lang Syne' have been used. Most successful of all, though, was 'Evening Hymn and Last Post', arranged by Dick Tulip of the Royal Fusiliers, which used as its base Sabine Baring-Gould's 'Now the Day Is Over'.

The popularity of these variations represented, in a quiet way, a change in the nature of remembrance. 'It must be a stony heart indeed which, hearing the Last Post, does not listen to it, is not moved by it, needs no furtive handkerchief,' wrote the journalist Colin Welch in 1983, but these were softer versions, more likely to provoke contemplation than tears. They lacked the harsh, gut-wrenching, naked emotion of the solo bugle, filtering the grief instead through melancholic sentiment.

And all the while, the forms of remembrance continued to be a source of dispute and disagreement and of political manoeuvring, sometimes in public, sometimes behind the scenes. Mostly this centred on the Cenotaph, and it was more often than not a result of politicians' reluctance to leave things alone.

Back in 1930 deep offence had been caused when the government proposed that foreign leaders on visits to Britain should not, as a matter of course, feel obliged to lay wreaths on the Cenotaph and the Tomb of the Unknown Warrior. The idea, it was said, was 'dictated by a desire not to continue to recall the terrible memories of the Great War', a sentiment that went down well in Berlin but was met with cries of outrage amongst Britain's allies, particularly in Belgium and America. In the face of the protests, there was a hurried clarification: 'It was pointed out that the constant fulfilment of this obligation was tending to cheapen by overuse a ceremony which ought to retain a particular significance.'

At that stage, any tampering with existing practice was almost bound to attract opposition. Forty-five years later, the question was less sensitive, sufficiently so that even the Remembrance Day service itself could be questioned. 'Clearly, as the wars become increasingly distant,' wrote Sir Arthur Peterson, permanent undersecretary at the home office, in a 1975 memo, 'some consideration ought to be given to the question whether the ceremony needs any alteration to take account of the passage of time – or perhaps even should be discontinued altogether.' That question was made more pertinent by a desire not to give offence to Britain's partners in the European Community, to which the country had recently been admitted. A committee, set up to look at the issue, considered the extreme option of abolition, as well as the milder choice of making some adjustments, such as ending the practice whereby a representative of each Commonwealth nation laid their own wreath on the Cenotaph; perhaps it would be sufficient, it was argued, to have just a single wreath, laid by the Queen.

In a country where the majority of the population still had a living memory of the Second World War, the committee's conclusion was – probably wisely – that the ceremony should remain, though 'if possible' it should be made 'more relevant'. The principal change that resulted, and which was implemented in 1980, was to extend the remit of the ceremony to include other bodies from outside the armed services who had suffered casualties during wartime, civilian services such as police officers and firefighters. The result proved uncontroversial and, where noticed, met with general approval.

So too did some subsequent developments. In 1998 the ranks of those taking part in the official parade were extended to include the Bevin Boys, survivors of the tens of thousands of young men conscripted to work in British coal mines as their contribution to the Second World War. Two years later, members of the First World War Pardon Association also joined, pursuing their campaign on behalf of those executed for alleged cowardice and desertion in the trenches. Also in 2000, 'Representatives of the Sikh, Buddhist, Hindu, Muslim and Greek Orthodox faiths joined Jewish and Christian leaders for the first time'. The service was still dominated by the established Church of England, but the concept of multi-faith inclusivity was modern Britain's equivalent of the absence of explicit religious meaning in the 1920s.

There were also many campaigning and protest groups who sought to use the Cenotaph to further their own agendas. On the 6th of August 1961, members of the Campaign for Nuclear Disarmament marked the anniversary of the bombing of Hiroshima by laying a wreath on the monument: 'A statement attached to the wreath linked Japanese civilians who died at Hiroshima with the allied soldiers killed while fighting the Japanese army,' remembered the poet Christopher Logue, who was one of the CND activists. Similarly in 1983 a wreath was laid by groups supporting the women encamped outside the RAF station at Greenham Common, protesting against the deployment there of American cruise missiles. 'It was clear from the inscription on the wreath that this was intended purely as a piece of propaganda,' the environment secretary, Tom King, told the cabinet. He argued that 'It was a longstanding convention that the national War Memorial should not be used for propaganda purposes of any kind,' and since the police had done nothing, because the wreath 'was not in their opinion offensive or liable to lead to a breach of the peace', he had taken matters into his own hands and had the wreath removed by staff from his department. Later that year, anti-cruise demonstrators were arrested after a demonstration at the monument.

From the other side of the political divide, there were marches on Remembrance Day in the 1960s by the Anglo-Rhodesian Society, supporting the white minority government of Ian Smith, and in the 1980s by members of the National Front and the British National Party, sometimes together and sometimes in rivalry. The latter groups came with a bugler to sound the Last Post and tried to stage a two minutes' silence, though more often than not, it simply provided an opportunity for noisy shouting from anti-fascist groups.

Considerably more offensive to many was the group objecting to the British government's policy on the Nigerian Civil War who interrupted the Silence at the Cenotaph in 1969 with shouts of 'Remember Biafra'. 'About eight young people were led along the pavement by police,' it was reported. 'There was some continued shouting and police clamped hands over the mouths of some people during the sounding of the Last Post.' In another time and another place, the Campaign for Homosexual Equality asked to be allowed to lay a wreath at the Remembrance Day ceremony in Wolverhampton in 1978. The Mayor permitted them to do so, and a number of other organisations promptly withdrew from the commemorations in protest.

What these various minor skirmishes reflected was not merely an attempt to exploit ceremonies for the purpose of gaining publicity for particular causes, but also a growing confusion about remembrance, an uncertainty about what it all meant in a modern Britain that had so little to do any more with the armed forces. There were still military involvements abroad, of course, and the civil war in Northern Ireland lasted for over a quarter of a century, reaching new depths of horror when the Remembrance Day commemoration in Enniskillen was bombed by the IRA in 1987, killing eleven people and wounding more than sixty. But no one born after the outbreak of war in 1939 had been subject to a military call-up, and the worlds of the civilian and the soldier were once more drifting apart. Cultural attitudes to what had formerly been spoken of proudly as 'the ultimate sacrifice' were shifting, perhaps irrevocably.

The nation that had once collectively vowed never to forget was becoming more casual about its past and its memories. In 1990 it was reported that when a church in Croydon was converted into an old people's home, a memorial slate was found in a builder's skip, bearing on it the names of some two hundred or so men from the area who had died in the First World War. The names had been painstakingly engraved in gold that they might live for all time, to be remembered and venerated by future generations, but now they had been deemed surplus to requirements. On discovery, the damaged and discarded slate was passed to the Imperial War Museum, though it was far from clear what could be done. 'When we wanted to put the names back in place,' a spokesperson for the Museum commented, 'it was pointed out that the old people at the home might not find them very cheerful.'

The same year, thanks to a ban on charity collections, the sale of poppies was stopped in Gloucestershire libraries. Meanwhile, attendance at Remembrance Day services continued to fall and, as some in the Church of England increasingly sought to distance themselves from the state, even the number of such ceremonies fell. 'Many of my clerical colleagues do not hold special services on the second Sunday in November,' lamented a Yorkshire vicar in 1982.

He was writing at a time when remembrance seemed in danger of becoming a charged political issue again, for Britain was now a deeply divided nation. The previous year, Michael Foot, the leader of the opposition Labour Party, had been mercilessly assaulted in the press for wearing what was wrongly called a donkey jacket to the Cenotaph service, even though it had met the approval on the day of the Queen Mother. ('That's a smart sensible coat for a day like this,' she had told him.) This time it was the turn of the newly formed Social Democratic Party to feel aggrieved, when their founder, Roy Jenkins, was not invited to join the leaders of other political parties in laying a wreath. But mostly Remembrance Day in 1982 was significant because it was held in the aftermath of the Falklands War, when the efficiency of the armed forces — in contrast to almost all other public services — had excited much admiration and approval. 'Congregations in the north of England were reported to be much higher because of the Falklands factor,' it was noted, 'and there were more young people attending services.'

Not everyone who attended, however, could be assumed to have been in support of the Falklands campaign. Tony Benn, the left-wing Labour MP for Bristol South East, who had served in the RAF during the Second World War, was seldom to be seen at Remembrance Day commemorations, but he made an appearance in Bristol that year. 'I wanted to be there because of the Falklands War,' he wrote. 'I am not prepared to concede to the Tories and the warmongers the sole right to remember the dead of war.'

That evening, an interview with the prime minister, Margaret Thatcher, was screened as part of the BBC programme *Songs of Praise*. The briefing note from her deputy press secretary suggested that she might want to take care with what she said: 'Clearly the Falklands will figure in your thoughts but I hope you agree that the Falkland factor should not be overplayed, especially at the expense of the more general feelings of Remembrance.' The concern was misplaced. For while Thatcher had never served in uniform, few prime ministers were quite so acutely sensitive to anything that involved the armed forces as she was. Despite the contemporary resonance of the Falklands, Remembrance Day in 1982 was no more politically charged than it had been in recent years.

Nonetheless, the intrusion of current events into remembrance was a continually thorny problem. At the Cenotaph service in 1990 a man set himself alight in protest at Britain's involvement in preparations for the war to liberate Kuwait, following that country's invasion by Saddam Hussein's Iraq. In response, the next year saw the introduction of intrusive security checks at the ceremony.

More controversial still was the service in 2001, just two months after the al-Qaeda attacks on the USA that killed nearly three thousand people, and one month after the start of the retaliatory bombing of Afghanistan. Such events could hardly be ignored. The prime minister, Tony Blair, let it be known that the wreath he was to lay would 'not only honour war heroes but the victims of the September 11th horror attacks'. Similarly, the Royal British Legion 'confirmed that the two-minute silence on Remembrance Sunday will also honour the lives of people killed on September 11th', though it was by no means clear that the Legion had the authority to determine the meaning of the Silence. Meanwhile the prime minister's press secretary, Alastair Campbell, was suggesting that Remembrance Day was 'a fitting time to explain why we are engaged' in bombing Afghanistan.

This was a very deliberate politicisation of remembrance and, as the British Army's involvement in Afghanistan was extended (it was to last longer than both world wars combined), and was joined by the invasion of Iraq in 2003, others felt justified in adding their own, dissenting voices. In 2005 the Serious Organised Crime and Police Act was passed, which included amongst its provisions a ban on unauthorised political demonstrations within a kilometre of the Houses of Parliament. The first prosecution came later that year when an anti-war campaigner stood at the Cenotaph and read out a list of the names of the ninety-seven British soldiers killed thus far in Iraq. Fourteen police officers apprehended her, and she was subsequently convicted and given a conditional discharge. 'My conviction sets a bit of a precedent,' she observed. 'It sends out the message that you will be arrested for remembering the dead.'

Yet all these episodes, by turns tragic, trivial and tawdry, even as they threatened to drag remembrance into the mire of politicking, could not entirely blunt the traditions. The Last Post remained sacred. It was heard at commemorations of the war, as when a group of former prisoners of war, survivors of the River Kwai, returned to pay their respects at Kanchanaburi War Cemetery in 1976, or when Jimmy Howe revisited the site of Stalag 8B to play in memory of his lost comrades. And it continued to be played at the funerals of old soldiers, though here it was largely dependent on the goodwill of individuals giving up their time, for there was no automatic right for an ex-serviceman in Britain to be given full military honours.

In America, on the other hand, such an entitlement was enshrined in law. By the beginning of the twenty-first century, this began to present a problem as the generation that fought in the Second World War neared the end of their lives. It was reported that, with some eighteen hundred veterans dying each day, and with only five hundred buglers in the US Army, it was becoming impossible to cope with the demand for the sounding of Taps by a serving member of the forces. The solution was found in automation: 'It is a bugle discreetly fitted with a battery-operated conical insert that plays the twenty-four notes of Taps at the flick of a switch,' marvelled the British press. 'It is all digital, with no human talent or breath required. All you do is hold it up, turn it on and try to look like a bugler.'

Despite everything that had changed since the Second World War, there was still a residual authority to the old calls. In 1993 the seventy-fifth anniversary of the Armistice was marked in Australia with the bringing home of a dead Australian serviceman from the fields of Flanders for re-burial as the Unknown Soldier. It was a ceremony of great solemnity, and in the wake of the 1986 Australia Act it felt as though the country – which had enjoyed only dominion status during the First World War – was asserting its nationhood by evoking its past: 'The Last Post sounded its wistful melancholy like delicate filigree in the air, its final notes giving way to silence on the eleventh hour of the eleventh day of the eleventh month.'

Further markers of time followed in quick succession: the eightieth anniversary of the outbreak of the First World War, the fiftieth anniversaries of D-Day, VE Day and VJ Day, and then in 1998 the eightieth anniversary of the Armistice. This was the last great commemoration at which survivors from the First World War were expected to be present, and it was duly honoured. In Paris, the Queen unveiled a statue to Winston Churchill, bearing the inscription 'We shall never surrender', before journeying to the Menin Gate. There a ceremony was held in which ten million poppy petals, representing the number of military deaths on both sides, fluttered down from the roof of the arch. It took a full five minutes for them all to fall.

This was the year too that the British Legion campaigned to have the Silence returned to its pre-1945 place in the calendar. The services at the Cenotaph and elsewhere were staged as usual on Remembrance Day, but then on Wednesday the 11th of November 1998, for the first time in over half a century, there came an Armistice Day Silence. Work on car production lines ceased, supermarkets suspended shopping, and buses, trains and planes came to a halt; trials at the Old Bailey stopped, as did activity in government offices, and Glasgow pubs opened two minutes later than normal. There was even a pause in Westminster, where the prime minister was being briefed on the consequences of the imminent bombing of Iraq: 'it was possible 2,500 people would die and UK planes and bombs would be responsible for about 250 of them.' Some forty-three million people, it was said, observed the Silence.

It was a surprisingly effective revival of a practice long thought to have disappeared. But it would have been foolish to assume that it meant the same as it had in 1945, let alone on that first anniversary in 1919, for it could not possibly have the same resonance. So much had changed since then. In the first place, the United Kingdom was not, a year after devolution referendums had been fought and won in Scotland and Wales, anywhere near as united as it once had been. 'The people of Ulster joined the English in honouring the dead,' noted historian Richard Weight, 'but those in the north and west of the mainland were less moved by what seemed to many an archaic ritual.' Even in England, old concepts of nationalism were becoming difficult to maintain in an era of globalisation: amongst those honouring the Silence were the Japanese-owned Nissan plant in Sunderland and the outlets of the German-owned retail chains Lidl and Aldi.

More than this, the vast majority of the population had no memory of life during wartime. George V's original wish that 'the thoughts of every one may be concentrated on reverent remembrance' was simply not applicable any more. Many could half-remember stories told them by parents and grandparents, and could berate themselves for not having listened more attentively. Others could conjure up an awareness of relatives they had never met, but whose names they had heard or had seen on a war memorial, mostly belonging to regiments that no longer existed. Some could even cast their minds to loved ones serving in uniform, though these were in a very small minority. There was no shared experience as there had been when remembrance had been part of the national culture, no common wellspring of suffering on which to draw.

And for that the country should have been deeply grateful. It was a luxury accorded to few civilisations in modern human history. In the space of two generations, peace had passed from being the normal, but by no means continuous, state of affairs to being taken for granted. That the Silence of 1998 was little more than a perfunctory, sentimental nod to history was an expression of the extraordinary good fortune enjoyed by those living in Western Europe in the second half of the twentieth century. Perhaps, eventually, one was tempted to reflect, 'lest we forget' truly had become 'never again'.

At the ceremony in Ypres that year, the 100-year-old veteran Arthur Halestrap, who had fought in France and whose son had died as a fighter pilot in the RAF, read Laurence Binyon's words – 'They shall grow not old' – and afterwards he spoke to the press. 'War was always a wicked thing,' he said. 'When I think of all the good men that were lost it makes me want to weep.' Also present was 101-year-old Robert Gelineau, who was even more concise: 'It was a useless war,' he said.

Contrary to expectations, however, 1998 was not the last great anniversary to retain a living link to 1914–18. Ten years later, Harry Patch, Henry Allingham and Bill Stone, of the Army, the Royal Air Force and the Royal Navy respectively, the final three men who had served in the conflict still alive in Britain, attended a service at the Cenotaph on the 11th of November 2008, the ninetieth anniversary of the Armistice. It was perhaps the only time when the smooth running of the ceremonial was interrupted.

The schedule called for the men, all three now in wheelchairs, to approach the monument, where their wreaths were to be taken from them by veterans of more recent wars and laid on the Cenotaph, after which the sounding of the Last Post would inaugurate the Silence. But the organisers had not allowed for the resilience of the ex-servicemen, and Henry Allingham was determined to lay his wreath himself, shuffling forward in his chair, struggling to rise from it, that he might personally honour his dead comrades. The chimes of Big Ben came and went as the 112-year-old man stubbornly continued his efforts to pay homage, the buglers looking nervously on as they awaited the order to play. Finally, he managed to lean far enough forward to place his wreath, and sank back in his wheelchair, as the Last Post rang out, two minutes later than planned.

A bugler of the Nottinghamshire (Sherwood Rangers) Yeomanry
sounds Reveille, 1939

REVEILLE

Trumpeter, what are you sounding now?
Is it the call I'm seeking?
'Lucky for you if you hear it at all
For my trumpet's but faint in speakin',
I'm callin' 'em home! Come home! Come home!
Tread light o'er the dead in the valley,
Who are lyin' around face down to the ground,
And they can't hear me sound the Rally.
But they'll hear it again in a grand refrain,
When Gabriel sounds the last Rally.'

John Francis Barron
'The Trumpeter' (1904)

O n the afternoon of Wednesday the 24th of January 1965, Basil King, the trumpet major of the Queen's Royal Irish Hussars, was playing football in Wolfenbüttel, Germany, when the orderly officer appeared on the touchline and called him over. He was told to put on a tracksuit and to report immediately to the colonel. Still wearing his football boots, covered in mud, and worrying that he was about to hear bad news concerning his family, King rushed to the colonel's office, where he was told to sit down. 'What I tell you now doesn't go past this room,' the colonel said. 'You're going to London on Saturday on the boat-train, and you'll be playing at Churchill's funeral.' 'But he's not dead,' protested King, and the colonel replied: 'He will be by Sunday.'

The colonel was right. When King landed at Harwich at breakfast time on Sunday morning, he was greeted with the news that Sir Winston Churchill, the former prime minister of the United Kingdom, had died at home, nine days after suffering a stroke. Seventy years earlier, Churchill had been commissioned as a junior officer in the 4th Queen's Own Hussars, who had subsequently been amalgamated to form the Queen's Royal Irish Hussars, of which he was the honorary colonel. Now the principal trumpeter of his old regiment had been summoned home to mark his death.

In London, Basil King was introduced to Corporal Peter Wilson of the Royal Horse Guards, one of the State Trumpeters. These were the two men selected to sound the Last Post and Reveille and, though no one else seemed much concerned as to who played which, neither was particularly keen on the Reveille, a long, complicated call that had greater potential for mistakes. They tossed a coin for it, and Wilson won. Situated up in the Whispering Gallery of St Paul's Cathedral, he would sound the Last Post; King, placed in the West Window, would play the Reveille. Both calls, in deference to Churchill's service career, were, of course, the cavalry versions.

The two men were very experienced trumpeters – while a pupil at Kneller Hall, King had played at the Queen's Coronation in 1953 – but this was an event of such weight and moment that the most skilled musician could be forgiven for feeling nervous about the possibility of fluffing his lines. There was even a recent precedent.

Fourteen months earlier the funeral had been staged at Arlington National Cemetery of President John F. Kennedy. The man chosen to play Taps on that occasion was Keith Clark, the principal bugler of the United States Army Band.

It was a freezing-cold day and Clark had to wait for three hours in the cemetery to do his duty to his former commander-in-chief. Worse yet, the demands of television meant that he was placed in front of the firing party, so that he had to play immediately after hearing three rifle volleys fired in close proximity. Perhaps unsurprisingly, his performance was not quite perfect; he failed to hit the sixth note in the call, a mistake broadcast to the nation and to the world. It was immediately seized upon by the American media as a symbol of the nation's grief over its murdered leader. 'The bugler's lip quivered for the nation,' was how it was reported, and the missed note was referred to as 'a tear'. Clark received a mass of letters, thanking him for his contribution: 'In your one sad note, you told the world of our feelings,' read one. 'It showed the tension that the nation felt,' was the verdict of Tom Sherlock, the senior historian at Arlington, many years later. 'It's part of the emotion. It's when a speech is well delivered and a voice cracks because it's an emotional time. It's what should happen. And in that way, it almost personalised it. And it made it immortal.'

Despite the accolades, it was not what Clark would have wished. 'I missed a note under pressure,' he reflected in later life. 'It's something you don't like, but it's something that can happen to a trumpet player. You never really get over it.'

Now Peter Wilson and Basil King were called upon to play at what the newspapers were referring to, perhaps justifiably, as 'the greatest funeral in world history'. The circumstances were very different from those of Kennedy's interment, but the potential for making a mistake was exactly the same. The funeral was being televised in Britain, where twenty-five million were to watch it, and around the world, where hundreds of millions more would join the audience.

For this, after all, was Winston Churchill, the man who had participated in the last great cavalry charge of the British Army, at the battle of Omdurman in the previous century; the man whose personal heroism during the Boer War would have won him a Victoria Cross had he still been in uniform rather than acting as a war correspondent; the man who had served in cabinet during the First World War and as prime minister during the Second World War. When he was born in 1874, Queen Victoria had yet to be proclaimed Empress of India; now the Empire was no more. For the best part of a century, he had embodied the history of the nation, had helped to make that history, and had written it afterwards.

As his body lay in state in Westminster Hall, more people came to pay their respects than had attended the last king, whilst others slept on the streets of London to ensure that they would bear witness to the funeral procession as it passed. Many of the hundreds of thousands who lined the streets were Londoners, but large numbers had travelled from other parts of the country and from beyond. 'We have come across specially to pay our respects,' said a man from Brittany, 'and now we will salute him with a farewell.'

Avoiding the worst of the crowds, Peter Wilson and Basil King arrived at St Paul's three hours before the service was scheduled to start, and began the long, nervous wait. 'It was a bit of an ordeal,' remembered King. 'We were professional musicians, but you've always got that bit of butterflies in the tummy because of the importance of it.'

They took their places in the cathedral shortly before the three thousand-strong congregation began to assemble — the politicians and heads of the armed forces, past and present, the official representatives of more governments than had ever previously met at such a gathering, the wartime allies and colleagues: Dwight D. Eisenhower, Ivan Koniev, Charles de Gaulle. More extraordinary still, there was the Queen, sitting with the Duke of Edinburgh and the Prince of Wales. State funerals for non-royals had been staged before, but never had the reigning monarch attended such an occasion, not even for the Duke of Wellington in 1852. The Queen's presence emphasised the profundity of the moment. When the service did commence, the intensity simply increased still further. 'I heard no sighs. I saw no tears,' wrote the *Daily Mirror*'s star columnist Cassandra. 'This was grief exultant.'

And then, after all the tributes had been paid and all the hymns had been sung – a fine, eclectic mixture that included 'The Battle Hymn of the Republic' as well as 'Oh God, Our Help in Ages Past' – it came down to just two solo trumpeters to articulate the emotions of the nation as it mourned the death of its greatest son, the most celebrated and feted leader of the free world. After an eternity of waiting, Peter Wilson's moment arrived, and he delivered a flawless Last Post, its clear tones echoing through the cathedral as though mourning the loss not simply of the man of Empire, but perhaps too of the Empire itself.

But the order of service at a soldier's funeral does not end with that call. 'The Last Post is the Nunc Dimittis of the dead soldier. It is the last bugle call,' Stephen Graham of the Scots Guards had written in 1919, before adding: 'It is the last, but it gives promise of Reveille – of the great Reveille which ultimately the Angel Gabriel ought to blow.' For if the Last Post speaks of grief and loss, then the Reveille offers faith in the resurrection and rebirth of the man, of the spirit and, in this instance, possibly even of the nation.

There came the two minutes' silence, two minutes of absolute stillness, timed to the second by the director of music of the Welsh Guards, as Basil King waited for his signal to play. 'I could look down and see all the royal family, all the cabinet and the high command, and I thought: God, don't muck this up,' he remembered. 'I fixed my gaze on some stone figure on the wall. And I played and it just went perfectly, no cracked notes or anything. Richard Dimbleby turned round and gave me the thumbs-up. It went right.'

'High up in the gallery,' reported the newspapers the next day, 'the Last Post echoing under the Dome and leaving on the air an incense of sound. Silence. And a single trumpeter's answering call – Reveille.'

REFERENCES

Prologue: The Last Post

Silent lie – from Edward Begbie, 'Remembrance', *Daily Chronicle* 11 November 1919

I believe – *Times* 7 November 1919

This is a people's war – *Times* 31 October 1914

In factories and workshops – *Times* 7 November 1919

might degenerate – *Derby Daily Telegraph* 12 November 1919

A disgusting idea – Nicolson, *The Great Silence* p. 142

Is daddy in there – *Hull Daily Mail* 12 November 1919

the only sound – *Dundee Courier* 12 November 1919

There was a loud detonation – *Manchester Guardian* 12 November 1919

The trams at the termini – *Hull Daily Mail* 11 November 1919

One man walked – *Manchester Guardian* 12 November 1919

the sounding of the siren – *Lichfield Mercury* 14 November 1919

the sudden hush – *Belfast Telegraph* 12 November 1919

one old gentleman – *Yorkshire Post and Leeds Intelligencer* 12 November 1919

entirely cut off – *Cheltenham Chronicle* 13 November 1920

Most of them – *Hull Daily Mail* 12 November 1919

the thoughts – *Times* 7 November 1919

It is a strong national trait – *Chelmsford Chronicle* 14 November 1919

both places – *Barrier Miner* 12 November 1919

It ended with a sigh – *Queensland Times* 15 November 1919

One of the most – *Swindon Advertiser and North Wilts Chronicle* 14 November 1919

The clergy – *Manchester Guardian* 12 November 1919

This touching spectacle – *Hull Daily Mail* 12 November 1919

Women cried freely – *Aberdeen Journal* 12 November 1919

Chapter One: Rouse

Their times – Josephus, *History of the Jewish War against the Romans*, book 3 chapter 5

This was to do – Custer, *Following the Guidon* p. xii

regulated by the sound – *Norfolk Chronicle* 5 April 1777

The movements – *Northampton Mercury* 21 September 1778

the buglers of his regiment – Fortescue, *The Last Post* p. 258

the Boers – *Western Gazette* 24 November 1899

to revise – *Journal of the Society for Army Historical Research* vol. 29 p. 19

Tattoo is divided – *Exeter Flying Post* 8 April 1863

There are altogether – *Otago Witness* 13 June 1885

All bugle calls – Graham, *A Private in the Guards* p. 106

buglers toured hostelries – *Yorkshire Evening Post* 14 October 1953

The Tattoo or First Post – *Otago Witness* 13 June 1885

the glorious 'grog' – Knight, *Marching to the Drums* p. 79

Get out of bed – sleeve notes to *Bugle Calls for the British Army* (Droit Music, 2002)

Officers' wives – Richards, *Old-Soldier Sahib* p. 160

At nine – *Manchester Guardian* 4 October 1854

To send the message – Knight, *Marching to the Drums* pp. 70–1

the most poetic – *The Graphic* 1 September 1894

the beautiful but weirdlike – *Yorkshire Gazette* 14 February 1885

The Reveille had sounded – Knight, *Marching to the Drums* p. 47

They are a body – Craik, MacFarlane, Knight, *The Pictorial History of England* p. 631

Our Commander-in-Chief – Knight, *Marching to the Drums* p. 195

The silence and gloom – *Times* 28 October 1854

Our men died – *Nottingham Evening Post* 3 December 1927

tribute of respect – *Fife Herald* 28 June 1855

affording a witness – *Times* 16 May 1856

It is a pleasing – *Leamington Spa Courier* 10 May 1856

the names of every – *Yorkshire Gazette* 3 March 1860

recording the names – *Dublin Evening Mail* 3 August 1864

That memorial windows – *London Standard* 27 September 1858

The present war – *Times* 5 May 1854

Chapter Two: General Salute

The day's high work – W.E. Henley, 'The Last Post', *For England's Sake*, 1900

a British gift – *Guardian* 10 April 1975

Few things – *Manchester Guardian* 9 May 1905

one of the most difficult – *Otago Daily Times* 31 October 1899

I heard the roll – *Hereford Journal* 18 April 1821

After the service – *Cheltenham Chronicle* 25 October 1864

the sudden sound – *Sussex Advertiser* 31 October 1865

disheartened – *Dumfries and Galloway Standard* 14 December 1853

the great body – *Dumfries and Galloway Standard* 2 November 1853

At the grave – *Newcastle Guardian and Tyne Mercury* 16 September 1871

ceremony closed – *Daily Gazette for Middlesbrough* 11 September 1871

before the grave – *Morpeth Herald* 14 July 1888

three volleys – *Gloucester Citizen* 10 December 1888

I could sound – Villanueva, *Twenty-Four Notes that Tap Deep Emotions* p. 7

The music was beautiful – ibid. p. 6

First of all – quoted in *Belfast News Letter* 29 August 1870

Flags were at half-mast – *Manchester Guardian* 19 May 1912

If you go into – *Leeds Times* 11 October 1856

they hated the Army – Laurie Dunn, interviewed by author

Women suffer – Henty, *Saint George for England*, chapter V

We don't want to fight – G.W. Hunt, 'MacDermott's War Song' (1878)

We aren't no – Rudyard Kipling, 'Tommy' (1892)

determined opposition – *Arbroath Herald and Advertiser for the Montrose Burghs* 26 January 1899

Old schoolfellows – E.W. Hornung, 'The Knees of the Gods' in *The Black Mask* (1901)

If ever a war – *Times* 7 October 1901

We have been unable – *San Francisco Call* 27 May 1900

surely they lived again – Knight, *Marching to the Drums* p. 291

After sounding – *San Francisco Call* 27 May 1900

ANOTHER WAR MEMORIAL – *Evening Post* 23 July 1904

who have recently fallen – *Manchester Guardian* 9 May 1903

The Last Post – Dooner, *The Last Post* p. vi

fine but somewhat thrasonical – *Spectator* 21 September 1901

simple but effective – Dibble, *Charles Villiers Stanford* p. 318

The effect – *Gloucester Citizen* 12 September 1900

scored an immediate success – *Advertiser* 16 October 1900

were seen – *Manchester Guardian* 28 November 1904

Chapter Three: Charge

Now, who are ye – from Maurice Hewlett, 'The Bugles', *The Toronto World* 7 February 1915

That there top note – *Spectator* 29 June 1917

perfectly shocked – *Manchester Guardian* 13 October 1914

everybody thought – *Western Daily Press* 10 October 1914

My third son – *Rothwell Courier & Times* 3 November 1919

the helmet – *Burnley News* 30 June 1915

both cried – *Evening Telegraph* 28 June 1915

I think of you — *Coventry Evening Telegraph* 5 April 1915

He always comes — *Yorkshire Post and Leeds Intelligencer* 8 January 1916

Here are huge cemeteries — Birmingham, *A Padre in France* p. 19

All through — *Aberdeen Journal* 7 October 1915

There are a good many — wwi.lib. byu.edu/index.php/The_Great_ War_Diaries_-_1918/1919_ (King%27s_African_Rifles) accessed 14 February 2014

The hospitals were full — *Spectator* 8 October 1936

I have no doubt — *Brisbane Courier* 20 September 1917

Having done — *Brisbane Courier* 21 September 1917

a country wagon — *Dundee Courier* 10 August 1914

Fourteen German soldiers — *Daily Mirror* 2 June 1915

There was no outburst — *Manchester Guardian* 7 September 1916

Even the enemy — Neave, *Remembering Kut* p. 72

the silver notes — *Weekly Times* 19 June 1915

The massed bands — *Manchester Guardian* 15 July 1916

The land that gave — E.S. Cohn, 'The Last Post', *World's News* 29 May 1915

No mournful sound — E. Coungeau, 'The Last Post', *Brisbane Courier* 26 May 1915

found in the pocket-book — *Mercury* 20 February 1917

It was one of — Buchan, *The History of the South African Forces in France* p. 273

in order to — http://www.salegion. co.za/two-minutes-silence.html accessed 14 February 2014

Eleven o'clock — *Manchester Guardian* 12 November 1918

up to the moment — *Times* 12 November 1918

which the peasantry — *Times* 12 November 1918

It's over, mate — *Aberdeen Evening Express* 12 November 1918

chubby little angels — *Manchester Guardian* 12 November 1918

In the West End — *Times* 12 November 1918

Chapter Four: Cease Firing

When with the morrow's dawn — *Punch* October 1917

mingled patriotic airs — *Burnley News* 13 November 1918

In almost every — *Manchester Guardian* 12 November 1918

one of these — *Western Daily Press* 13 November 1918

a band marched — *Hastings and St Leonards Observer* 16 November 1918

followed by — *Nottingham Evening Post* 13 November 1918

and the crowd — *Coventry Evening Telegraph* 14 November 1918

mixed but vigorous — *Times* 18 November 1918

It is undesirable – *Observer* 17 November 1918

eight abreast – *Times* 25 November 1918

Are we downhearted – *Taunton Courier and Western Advertiser* 27 November 1918

Many eyes – *Cheltenham Chronicle* 30 November 1918

Thousands of men – ibid.

For God's sake – *Liverpool Echo* 27 November 1918

a loyal frenzy – *Times* 25 November 1918

We want no – *Observer* 17 November 1918

If a counterblast – *Aberdeen Journal* 25 November 1918

Where *is* this land – Nicolson, *The Great Silence* p. 72

What is our task? – *Times* 25 November 1918

a sullen unresponsiveness – Nicolson, *The Great Silence* p. 72

It dawned on me – ibid. p. 73

The man who won – quoted in *Manchester Guardian* 9 December 1918

majestic and moving – *Spectator* 18 July 1919

The dominant note – *Times* 14 July 1919

in the form of – *Times* 5 July 1919

Sunlight glinting – *Yorkshire Evening Post* 14 July 1919

a point of homage – Nicolson, *The Great Silence* p. 109

not a catafalque – Hussey, *The Life of Sir Edwin Lutyens* p. 392

Keenotaph – Jenkins, *The Twenties* p. 12

All religions – Winter, *Sites of Memory, Sites of Mourning* p. 103

simple classical cenotaph – *Manchester Guardian* 21 July 1919

The Cenotaph – Hussey, *The Life of Sir Edwin Lutyens* p. 392

a life – Nicolson, *The Great Silence* p. 265

This time there were – *Derby Daily Telegraph* 21 July 1919

this seems finer still – *Manchester Guardian* 21 July 1919

shouted themselves hoarse – *Derby Daily Telegraph* 21 July 1919

Had he not done so – *Manchester Guardian* 21 July 1919

the centre of which – *Manchester Guardian* 19 July 1919

It was a merry scene – *Times* 21 July 1919

stillness that was – *Aberdeen Journal* 21 July 1919

this sacred point – *Manchester Guardian* 21 July 1919

Old English dances – *Aberdeen Journal* 21 July 1919

Rockets went up – *Western Daily Press* 21 July 1919

It was a solemn moment – *Dundee Courier* 21 July 1919

Sir Edwin Lutyens's design – *Times* 21 July 1919

Germanic – Winter, *Sites of Memory, Sites of Mourning* p. 103

When the other – *Spectator* 20 November 1920

The Monument – memo dated 23 July 1919, National Archives CAB/24/84

the human sentiment – National Archives, WORK/20/226

A mass of – memo dated 15 October 1919, National Archives CAB 24/GT8335

The souls of the righteous – *Times* 28 July 1919

There is no room – *Times* 26 July 1919

extremely likely – memo dated 8 December 1919, National Archives CAB/24/94

Passengers in the streets – *Chelmsford Chronicle* 26 July 1918

If this can be done – quoted in *Chelmsford Chronicle* 18 October 1918

Can we not spare – quoted in *Yorkshire Evening Post* 11 November 1929

the fact that the custom – *Times* 20 November 1925

Silence, complete – memo dated 4 November 1919, National Archives CAB 24/CP45

The King – *Manchester Guardian* 26 January 1931

There is left behind – *Derby Daily Telegraph* 12 November 1919

An unknown British Soldier – *Times* 1 July 1955

Let this body – *Times* 15 November 1980

A thing that appeals – *Times* 30 October 1919

poised precariously – Nicolson, *The Great Silence* pp. 266–7

one false move – John Preston, *Sunday Telegraph* 9 November 2008

cremated – cabinet minutes 15 October 1920, National Archives CAB/23/22

something more martial – Dean & Turner, *Sound the Trumpets* p. 14

We want simplicity – *Nottingham Evening Post* 27 June 1924

stiff-necked clergy – *Western Gazette* 6 August 1926

predecessors had tried – *Gloucester Journal* 7 August 1926

young people – *Aberdeen Journal* 7 August 1928

But that was the Church's loss – *Times* 8 July 1955

sometimes being requisitioned – *Tamworth Herald* 20 November 1920

a bucket – *Daily Telegraph* 10 November 2006

would do honour – memo to cabinet 15 October 1920, National Archives CAB/23/22

to the English mind – *Observer* 13 November 1921

is a far more – *Manchester Guardian* 15 November 1921

We cannot hope – Blythe, *The Age of Illusion* p. 12

unaccompanied – *Times* 20 June 1946

Mohammedans – Gregory, *The Silence of Memory* p. 187

has become a national shrine –
    Hussey, *The Life of Sir Edwin Lutyens*
    p. 394
We are prepared – *Manchester
    Guardian*, 10 November 1920
Five days after its unveiling
    – *Spectator* 20 November 1920
solemn pilgrimage – *Observer*
    28 November 1920
you could walk – *Manchester Guardian*
    15 November 1920

Chapter Five: Alarm

Shrieking upon – from Eric
    Wearing, 'Last Post (The Marine
    Barracks, Chatham)', *Western
    Morning News* 19 August 1931
Those trumpets called – *Observer*
    22 November 1914
tribute to – *Grantham Journal*
    24 November 1900
symbolising the tragic end – *Hastings
    and St Leonards Observer*
    8 November 1919
London Road – *Times* 5 August 1919
The police opened fire – quoted in
    Hull Daily Mail 23 July 1919
only one out of – *Times* 29 May 1919
The Army is disaffected – Davies,
    To Build a New Jerusalem p. 87
A servants' festival – Nicolson, *The
    Great Silence* p. 108
General's widow – *Dundee Courier*
    5 August 1919
Honour the dead – *Manchester
    Guardian* 21 July 1919
deplorable scenes – *Taunton Courier
    and Western Advertiser* 23 July 1919

proceeded to break – *Dundee Courier*
    21 July 1919
the mob took possession – *Derby
    Daily Telegraph* 21 July 1919
There was no lack – *Western Daily Press*
    23 July 1919
a mob of men – *Western Times* 22 July
    1919
at considerable expense – *Hull Daily
    Mail* 23 July 1919
vigorously stoned – *Evening Telegraph*
    22 July 1919
The tendency – *Derby Daily Telegraph*
    23 July 1919
Strikers belonging – *Evening Telegraph*
    12 November 1919
a large body – *Western Gazette*
    30 September 1921
not only destitute – *Manchester
    Guardian* 31 January 1921
a number of men – *Times* 4 January
    1921
They came back – Dennis, *The Last
    Post* p. 15
I dressed myself – *Hull Daily Mail*
    21 November 1921
My conviction – *Nottingham Evening
    Post* 21 November 1921
whilst living heroes – *Western Daily
    Press* 12 November 1920
While the great pageant – *Daily
    Herald* 11 November 1920
The dead are remembered – *Times*
    12 November 1921
Bread – *Dundee Courier* 12 November
    1921
a violent babel – *Evening Telegraph*
    11 November 1921

What we want — *Yorkshire Post and Leeds
Intelligencer* 12 November 1921
The red flag — *Dundee Courier* 12
November 1921
To those who died — *Western Times*
12 November 1921
To the victims — *Dundee Courier*
12 November 1921
Girls seemed to be dancing
— *Manchester Guardian*
12 November 1920
We were dusting — *Cheltenham
Chronicle* 13 November 1920
being used as a platform — *Observer*
28 November 1920
Why all these demands? — *Manchester
Guardian* 12 November 1924
a young man — *Nottingham Evening Post*
12 November 1928
to provoke an outbreak — *Times*
30 May 1919
the agents — *Exeter and Plymouth Gazette*
10 January 1921
Our Glorious Living — *Daily Express*
10 November 1927
chief mourner — *Times* 12 November
1920
Today's act — *Dundee Courier*
12 November 1926
I felt that — *Daily Mail* 12 November
1927
Ex-service men — *Aberdeen Journal*
23 February 1920
got together — *Tamworth Herald*
27 September 1919
The ex-Service Associations —
National Archives CAB/24/129
loyalty, unity — *Times* 13 November
1923

the Legion had saved — *Times*
14 December 1926
Unless — Shinwell, *Lead with the Left*
p. 72

Chapter Six: Fall In

Solemn the drums — from
Laurence Binyon, 'For the
Fallen', *Times* 21 September 1914
the wearing of — *Times* 6 October
1921
On every memorial — *Manchester
Guardian* 8 November 1921
Clumps of crimson — Saunders, *The
Poppy* p. 68
Take up our quarrel — from John
McCrae, 'In Flanders Fields',
Punch 8 December 1915
these were not — *Times* 24 November
1921
often inadequate — *Times*
11 November 1925
almost universal — *Manchester Guardian*
12 November 1924
will become — memo dated
13 October 1921, National
Archives CAB/24/129
That, surely — *Times* 16 November
1922
should consult — cabinet minutes
26 September 1923, National
Archives CAB/23/46
This should not prejudice — cabinet
minutes 15 October 1923,
National Archives CAB/23/46
eloquent and energetic — *Aberdeen
Journal* 3 November 1923
This by no means — *Derby Daily
Telegraph* 22 October 1923

an annual custom – *Dundee Courier*
19 October 1923

amazingly fatuous – *Western Daily Press*
24 October 1923

Admission will be – *Yorkshire Post and
Leeds Intelligencer* 20 October 1923

It makes you shiver – *Manchester
Guardian* 12 November 1923

Those who went to church – *Daily
Express* 12 November 1919

prepared to make – *Yorkshire Post and
Leeds Intelligencer* 20 October 1923

strong public opinion – cabinet
minutes 22 October 1923,
National Archives CAB/23/46

it might be difficult – *Observer*
21 October 1923

a pagan flower – Saunders, *The Poppy*
p. 68

deeply impressed – *Times*
23 October 1923

So soon as – memo dated 16 April
1928, National Archives
CAB/24/194

considerably revised – *Gloucester
Citizen* 12 November 1923

the most striking – *Times*
12 November 1925

It was felt – memo dated 16 April
1928, National Archives
CAB/24/194

mechanical contrivances – *Times*
3 November 1927

Assuming – Thomas, *The Establishment*
p. 178

You state that – letter dated
29 October 1924, National
Archives HO4/11557

The public demand – memo dated
16 April 1928, National
Archives CAB/24/194

The picture – *Times* 12 November
1928

Tomorrow at dawn – *Daily News*
(Perth) 6 February 1918

The vocal people – Buchan, *The
Dancing Floor* chapter 3

The decision – *Dundee Courier*
31 October 1929

The sudden revival – *Times*
10 December 1929

Chapter Seven: Stand Fast

The Last Post – from Mollie
Kremer, 'The Last Post Calls',
Sydney Morning Herald 25 April 1935

The war has been over – *Sunday
Express* 7 November 1926

where all the men – Mee, *Enchanted
Land* p. 144

a playground – *Spectator* 16 April
1920

all who served – Winter, *Sites of
Memory, Sites of Mourning* p. 98

All men are equal – *Montreal Gazette*
25 May 1936

at the present time – *Cornishman*
8 June 1916

with equal readiness – *Sydney Morning
Herald* 4 August 1933

I maintain – *Rothwell Courier & Times*
4 November 1919

largest bit – Gilmour, *The Long
Recessional* p. 281

privilege in the face – ibid. p. 279

It used to be said – *Spectator*
19 November 1927

Many prophesied — *Essex Newsman* 8 November 1930

Each year — *Manchester Guardian* 12 November 1932

Last Post was — Dean, *Jiggs* p. 132

its sweeping — *Times* 4 August 1932

the singing — *Manchester Guardian* 10 November 1934

In remembrance — *Manchester Guardian* 12 November 1923

By the sacred memory — *Daily Herald* 11 November 1919

The purpose — memo dated 24 September 1929, National Archives CAB/24/206

really a peace celebration — Gregory, *The Silence of Memory* p. 124

if you wish — *Daily Mail* 11 November 1930

peace teaching — *Times* 9 November 1937

Once again — *Hull Daily Mail* 11 September 1933

It is held — *Spectator* 19 November 1927

Every theatre — *Sydney Morning Herald* 14 November 1919

Quite frankly — Nicolson, *The Great Silence* p. 149

In the morning — *Times* 7 November 1921

Imperceptibly, the Feast-Day — Gregory, *The Silence of Memory* p. 65

Thousands were moved — quoted in *Observer* 17 October 1926

Is it dreadfully — *Times* 20 October 1925

it is better — *Daily Mail* 23 October 1925

Personally, I would — *Daily Mail* 24 October 1925

during the last week — *Times* 5 November 1925

the like of which — *Times* 12 November 1927

could shout — *Times* 12 November 1929

We renounce war — *Manchester Guardian* 16 October 1934

No Christian man — *Manchester Guardian* 28 May 1934

There is no — *Nottingham Evening Post* 26 November 1935

instead of the customary bugle — *Times* 12 November 1937

those who consider — *Portsmouth Evening News* 5 December 1938

We believe as pacifists — *Nottingham Evening Post* 24 January 1939

To us they were notes — *Guardian* 10 April 1975

German as well — *Spectator* 22 August 1930

It is emphatically — *Western Morning News* 1 February 1930

The Last Post — *Glasgow Herald* 25 September 1930

This is being done — *Gloucester Citizen* 25 September 1930

It is a lonely — *Auckland Star* 10 June 1939

has announced — *Western Morning News* 18 July 1935

the Last Post — *Aberdeen Journal* 11 July 1938

Every night — *Times* 18 January 1936

at sunset — *Dundee Courier* 17 February 1931

Chapter Eight: As You Were

There is a sound – from J. Tyler, 'Armistice Day', *Western Mail* 9 November 1939

The white tall pillars – Middelboe, Fry & Grace, *We Shall Never Surrender* p. 28

Year after year – *Yorkshire Post and Leeds Intelligencer* 11 November 1940

Mother and I – Smith, *These Wonderful Rumours!* p. 53

proud bereavement – Gregory, *The Silence of Memory* p. 35

Why bother – *Bath Chronicle and Weekly Gazette* 15 November 1941

in our hearts – *Observer* 10 November 1940

Owing to the risk – *Exeter and Plymouth Gazette* 8 November 1940

there was less – *Gloucestershire Echo* 9 November 1942

Here we are – *Morpeth Herald* 10 November 1944

Remembrance Day – Smith, *These Wonderful Rumours!* p. 246

Of late – *Times* 8 November 1944

The one thing – *Mrs Milburn's Diaries* p. 309

During the silence – *Derby Daily Telegraph* 12 November 1940

broadcast from – *Times* 12 November 1940

would be glad – *Manchester Guardian* 11 November 1940

Perhaps someone's daddy – *Dundee Courier* 13 September 1940

If it is a choice – *Spectator* 27 February 1941

He was given – Howe, *A Conductor's Journey* p. 38

the Last Post – *Auckland Star* 27 September 1944

Day after day – *Kalgoorlie Miner* 11 December 1942

in commemoration – home office memo, 12 July 1945, National Archives CAB/66/67/27

the sudden – *Manchester Guardian* 11 November 1946

before boarding – *New Zealand Herald* 13 November 1945

They are afraid – *The Mercury* 12 November 1945

The Two Minutes Silence – *Times* 8 November 1946

folksongs and laments – Gregory, *The Silence of Memory* p. 128

of Albert Collins – *Western Gazette* 28 September 1945

one for 1914 – Gregory, *The Silence of Memory* p. 173

If anyone – Garfield, *Our Hidden Lives* p. 464

was not unmarred – *Manchester Guardian* 8 November 1948

The fact that – *West London Observer* 12 November 1954

They stood – *Courier-Mail* 11 November 1946

I have no time – Garfield, *Our Hidden Lives* p. 123

this national cadging – *Manchester Guardian* 9 March 1949

the greatest – *Times* 12 December 1949

the utter failure – Attlee, *The Social Worker* p. 10

collective – ibid. p. 12

for Legion charity – *Manchester
Guardian* 14 November 1949

The Legion – *Manchester Guardian*
11 January 1949

The victory – *Times* 9 May 1985

the income to pay – *Manchester
Guardian* 10 October 1947

Chapter Nine: Dismiss

Did they beat – Eric Bogle, 'No
Man's Land' (Larrikin Music
Pty Limited, 1976)

I still felt a tug – Blair, *A Journey*
p. 126

and for the final – *The Age* 2 April
1976

The Last Post – *Sydney Morning Herald*
11 June 1984

For fifty-odd years – *Independent*
3 December 1998

his comrades – *Manchester Guardian*
1 October 1917

Messages of solidarity – *Guardian*
19 April 1976

designed as – *The Nation* 8 November
1997

I'd like to be – *Spokane Daily Chronicle*
7 June 1958

conveying a Wagnerian – *Bath
Chronicle and Weekly Gazette*,
25 March 1939

It must be a stony heart – *Spectator*
12 November 1983

dictated by – *Manchester Guardian*
24 October 1930

It was pointed out – *Times*
25 October 1930

Clearly, as the wars – *Daily Telegraph*
29 December 2005

if possible – *Daily Mirror*
29 December 2005

Representatives of – *Guardian*
13 November 2000

A statement – *Guardian* 28 August
1999

It was clear – cabinet minutes,
10 March 1983, National
Archives CAB/128/76/8

About eight – *Guardian*
10 November 1969

When we wanted – *Times*
10 November 1990

Many of my – *Guardian* 13 November
1982

That's a smart – Morgan, *Michael
Foot* p. 391

Congregations – *Times* 15 November
1982

I wanted to be there – Benn, *The End
of an Era* p. 255

Clearly the Falklands – minute
dated 20 October 1982,
Churchill Archive Centre
THCR 1/4/6 part 1 f3

not only honour – *Daily Mirror*
10 November 2001

confirmed that – *Express*
10 November 2001

a fitting time – *Evening Standard*
12 November 2001

My conviction – *Evening Standard*
8 December 2005

It is a bugle – *Guardian* 27 September
2003

The Last Post – *Canberra Times*
12 November 1993

it was possible — Campbell, *The Blair Years* pp. 331-2

The people of Ulster — Weight, *Patriots* p. 669

War was always — *Sun* 12 November 1998

It was a useless war — *Guardian* 12 November 1998

Epilogue: Reveille

Trumpeter — from 'The Trumpeter', words by John Francis Barron, music by J. Airlie Dix

What I tell you — Basil King, interviewed by author

The bugler's lip — *TV Guide* 25 January 1964

a tear — tapsbugler. com/a-bugle-call-remembered, accessed 12 March 2014

It showed — *New York Times* 17 January 2002

I missed a note — Associated Press, 22 November 1988

the greatest funeral — Cassandra, *At His Finest and Funniest* p. 133

We have come — *Canberra Times* 1 February 1965

I heard no sighs — Cassandra, *At His Finest and Funniest* p. 134

The Last Post — Graham, *A Private in the Guards* p. 101

High up — *Observer* 31 January 1965

BIBLIOGRAPHY

Note: Much of the material included in this book, as will be apparent from the references, is drawn from the newspapers of the time, but the following books have also been consulted. Where a paperback or revised edition is shown, it indicates that any page references are to that edition.

David Ascoli, *A Companion to the British Army 1660–1983* (George Harrap, 1983)

C.R. Attlee, *The Social Worker* (G. Bell and Sons, 1920)

Hugh Barty-King, *The Drum: A Royal Tournament Tribute to the Military Drum* (Royal Tournament, 1988)

Tony Benn (ed. Ruth Winstone), *The End of an Era: Diaries 1980–90* (Hutchinson, 1992 – pbk edn: Arrow, 1994)

George A. Birmingham, *A Padre in France* (Hodder & Stoughton, 1919)

Tony Blair, *A Journey* (Hutchinson, 2010)

Ronald Blythe, *The Age of Illusion: Glimpses of Britain between the Wars 1919–1940* (Hamish Hamilton, 1963 – pbk edn: Oxford University Press, 1983)

John Brophy and Eric Partridge, *The Long Trail: Soldiers' Songs and Slang 1914–18* (Andre Deutsch, 1965)

John Buchan, *The History of the South African Forces in France* (Thomas Nelson & Sons, 1920)

John Buchan, *The Dancing Floor* (Hodder & Stoughton, 1926)

David Butler and Anne Sloman, *British Political Facts 1900–1979* (fifth edition, Macmillan, 1980)

Alastair Campbell and Richard Stott (eds), *The Blair Years: Extracts from the Alastair Campbell Diaries* (Hutchinson, 2007)

Cassandra, *At His Finest and Funniest* (Paul Hamlyn, 1967)

Elizabeth B. Custer, *Following the Guidon* (Harper & Brothers, 1895)

A.J. Davies, *To Build a New Jerusalem: The Labour Movements from the 1880s to the 1990s* (Michael Joseph, 1992)

Colin Dean, *Jiggs: A Biography of Lieutenant-Colonel C.H. Jaeger OBE* (Parapress, 2013)

Colin Dean and Gordon Turner (eds), *Sound the Trumpets, Beat the Drums: Military Music through the 20th Century* (Parapress, 2002)

James Dennis, *The Last Post* (Lancaster Military Heritage Group, 2006)

Jeremy Dibble, *Charles Villiers Stanford: Man and Musician* (OUP, 2002)

Peter Donnelly (ed.), *Mrs Milburn's Diaries: An Englishwoman's Day-to-Day Reflections 1939–45* (George Harrap, 1979 – pbk edn: Fontana, 1981)

Mildred G. Dooner, *The 'Last Post': Being a Roll Call of all Officers (Naval, Military or Colonial) Who Gave Their Lives for Their Queen, King and Country in the South African War 1899–1902* (Simpkin, Marshall, Hamilton & Kent, 1903)

Henry George Farmer, *The Rise and Development of Military Music* (William Reeves, 1912)

John W. Fortescue, *The Last Post* (Blackwood, 1934)

Simon Garfield, *Our Hidden Lives: The Remarkable Diaries of Post-War Britain* (Ebury Press, 2004 – pbk edn: Random House, 2005)

David Gilmour, *The Long Recessional: The Imperial Life of Rudyard Kipling* (John Murray, 2002)

Stephen Graham, *A Private in the Guards* (Macmillan, 1919)

Robert Graves, *Fairies and Fusiliers* (Heinemann, 1917)

Adrian Gregory, *The Silence of Memory: Armistice Day 1919–1946* (Berg, 1994)

Mike Hall, *With Trumpet, Drum and Fife* (Helion & Company, 2013)

W.E. Henley, *For England's Sake: Verses and Songs in Time of War* (Constable, 1900)

G.A. Henty, *Saint George for England: A Tale of Cressy and Poitiers* (Dean & Son, 1885)

Ian Hernon, *Riot! Civil Insurrection from Peterloo to the Present Day* (Pluto, 2006)

Jimmy Howe, *A Conductor's Journey* (JH Publishing, 2002)

Michael Hurd, *Soldiers' Songs and Marches* (Oxford University Press, 1966)

Christopher Hussey, *The Life of Sir Edwin Lutyens* (Country Life, 1950 – new edn: Antique Collectors Club, 1984)

Alan Jenkins, *The Twenties* (William Heinemann, 1974)

Ian Knight, *Marching to the Drums: From the Kabul Massacre to the Siege of Mafeking* (Greenhill Books, 1999)

Arthur Mee, *Enchanted Land: Half-a-Million Miles in the King's England* (Hodder & Stoughton, 1936)

Penelope Middelboe, Donald Fry & Christopher Grace, *We Shall Never Surrender: Wartime Diaries 1939–1945* (Macmillan, 2011 – pbk edn: Pan, 2012)

Kenneth O. Morgan, *Michael Foot: A Life* (HarperCollins, 2007)

Dorina Neave, *Remembering Kut: Lest We Forget* (Arthur Barker, 1937)

Juliet Nicolson, *The Great Silence 1918–1920: Living in the Shadow of the Great War* (John Murray, 2009)

Punch magazine, *Mr Punch's History of the Great War* (Cassell & Co, 1919)

Frank Richards, *Old-Soldier Sahib* (Faber & Faber, 1936)

Jeffrey Richards, *Imperialism and Music: Britain 1876–1953* (Manchester University Press, 2001)

Nicholas J. Saunders, *The Poppy: A Cultural History from Ancient Egypt to Flanders Fields to Afghanistan* (Oneworld, 2013)

Gary Sheffield, *The Chief: Douglas Haig and the British Army* (Aurum, 2011 – pbk edn: 2012)

Manny Shinwell, *Lead with the Left: My First Ninety-Six Years* (Cassell, 1981)

May Smith (ed. Duncan Marlor), *These Wonderful Rumours! A Young Schoolteacher's Wartime Diaries 1939–1945* (Virago, 2012)

Hugh Thomas (ed.), *The Establishment* (Anthony Blond, 1959 – pbk edn: Ace Books, 1962)

Gordon Turner and Alwyn W. Turner, *The History of British Military Bands Volume 1: Cavalry and Corps* (Spellmount, 1994)

Gordon Turner and Alwyn W. Turner, *The History of British Military Bands Volume 2: Guards and Infantry* (Spellmount, 1996)

Gordon Turner and Alwyn W. Turner, *The History of British Military Bands Volume 3: Infantry and Irish* (Spellmount, 1997)

Jari Villanueva, *Twenty-Four Notes that Tap Deep Emotions* (JV Music, 2011)

Richard Weight, *Patriots: National Identity in Britain 1940–2000* (Macmillan, 2002 – pbk edn: Pan, 2003)

Patty Old West, *Good and Faithful Servant: Remembering Ken Old, Missionary to Pakistan* (Tate Publishing, 2010)

Ross J. Wilson, *Cultural Heritage of the Great War in Britain* (Ashgate, 2013)

Jay Winter, *Sites of Memory, Sites of Mourning: The Great War in European Cultural History* (Cambridge University Press, 1995)

ACKNOWLEDGEMENTS

As ever, I am indebted to a number of people who shared their memories and thoughts, or who helped and encouraged this project, including: Basil King, Brian Freeborn, Dan Atkinson, Eric Bogle, Havana Marking, Herbert Iredell, Hugh Levinson, Hugo Frey, Ian Connerty, Ian Sherwood, Jackie Loos, Jari Villanueva, Jenny de Tolly, Laurie Dunn, Martin Herring, Nina Antonia, Peter Francis, Richard Powell, Ross Wilson, Steve Mason and Stan Patch.

I'm grateful for the assistance of Colin Dean, who knows more about military music than I ever shall, and of my father Gordon Turner, who has answered my persistent questions with great tolerance and insight.

This is the sixth book I've written that has been published by Aurum Press and I continue to admire their enthusiasm and efficiency. My thanks to Charlotte Coulthard, Jessica Axe and Lucy Warburton, as well as to the excellent cover designer Leo Nickolls and the equally excellent text editor Steve Gove. And most especially to Sam Harrison, formerly of this parish, who really is a terrifically good editor. This book has been more pleasurable to write than any other, and a large part of that is thanks to him.

Finally, my gratitude to Thamasin Marsh for living through this project with me and for providing support.

INDEX

Page numbers in *italic* refer to captions

N°. 35. TATTOO. *(Last Post.)*